A FAILURE OF NERVE IN 52 WEEKS

EDWIN H. FRIEDMAN

A Failure of Nerve
in 52 Weeks

A Yearlong Leadership Planner

Morehouse Publishing
NEW YORK

Morehouse Publishing
19 East 34th Street
New York, NY 10016
www.churchpublishing.org

Morehouse Publishing is an imprint of Church Publishing Incorporated.

Original cover design by Stefan Killen; revised by Jennifer Kopec, 2Pug Design

ISBN 978-1-64065-652-9 (paperback)

CONTENTS

HOW TO USE THIS BOOK

Today's leaders must operate in the face of a society defined by emotional regression, overwhelming data flows, and a history of sabotage towards independent actors. Yet a well-differentiated leader is exactly what is necessary to reclaim the spirit of adventure that drove the Age of Discovery and unlock the opportunities the future holds.

This is a book that will help you to become one such leader.

Each week focuses on a core tenant from Edwin H. Friedman's *A Failure of Nerve: Leadership in the Age of the Quick Fix*. Brief excerpts of his wisdom are paired with either:

- **True/False questions to test your comprehension or highlight an aspect of your leadership style**
- **Scales to gauge the severity of a situation or belief**
- **Word matrices to emphasize concepts and test memory**
- **Reflection questions to stimulate self-analysis and promote future planning**

Other features include a planning page with space for daily appointments, goals, and reflections. The "thought for the week" highlights a guiding principle or provocative statement from Friedman's work.

We recommend reading and engaging with this planner weekly—after all, true leadership doesn't develop overnight. However, if life gets in the way, the book's flexible design allows for you to pick *A Failure of Nerve in 52 Weeks* back up at any time to continue your journey. You'll be glad you did.

Imaginative, self-defined leadership awaits.

FOREWORD

Anxiety and the search for rapid solutions always result in a failure of nerve. Needing to be right, certain, and pain free, we narrow our thinking and put our courage on pause. Operating from a quick-fix mentality is a non-growth position. Instead, Edwin Friedman proposes that challenge is necessary for mature functioning.

I know this from personal experience. I remember the day vividly. I was stunned. The audiologist told me that I had "sudden hearing loss," something brought on by bronchitis, a severe cold, or an upper respiratory disorder. It started one afternoon while I was talking to a friend who suddenly sounded like Donald Duck. For the next few days, I thought the clogging of my left ear was a temporary state. But when it persisted, I arranged for a visit with the specialist, who delivered the news. So there I was, two weeks before Christmas, sitting in my home breathing in a substance from a tank every twenty minutes, the crude but only known treatment. I was told that there was little chance I would regain hearing in that ear. I was depressed. My two daughters were home from college for Christmas break and tried to be "the comforters of Job" on my behalf, assuring me. They noted that my right ear was performing well, that I could overcome this adversity, and that a new remedy might appear soon.

The following month I went to Bethesda, Maryland, for the second of three training events with Dr. Friedman, which he called the Post Graduate Seminar in Family Emotional Functioning. In order to hear well, I arrived early and took a front seat. Dr. Friedman was busy setting up the room for the 2 o'clock start. I told him about my hearing loss and my daughters' efforts to console me. "I can't even suffer in my own family," I lamented. Dr. Friedman continued with the set-up, but then came to me and said, "Looks like you helped to form this system. What are you going to do about it?" As you can imagine, I did not expect a question about my own functioning. But as Friedman often noted, "questions subvert mindsets." I was not a victim, incompetent, or a helpless person. If anything, I had been a "co-conspirator" in my own family process of dousing pain.

The following day, Rabbi Friedman introduced the class to his formula in the structure of a fraction:

$$HE \over RO$$

HE represented the number and strengths of the stressors, while RO stood for the response of the organism. My RO, I realized, was more important than the condition of hearing loss. As the denominator, my "response" could undo or topple the "hostility of the environment." It is no wonder that I stayed in the training for another seven years.

Friedman's legacy is secure; *A Failure of Nerve* is sound proof of that. Countless individuals and groups have been challenged to increase their RO and to have the courage to deal with their bruises and burdens, relationship tensions, and a host of hostile forces. I have played a small part in the legacy, training clergy in Bowen Family Systems Theory (which Friedman used to clarify his own thinking), intervening in hundreds of conflicted systems, both large and small, and attending to my own functioning. This tenth anniversary edition of *A Failure of Nerve* extends the legacy for many more individuals and systems.

Trained as a rabbi, Friedman was at ease with metaphors, images, aphorisms, and narratives, since Midrash was an essential element in rabbinical interpretation. He enriched his writing by plumbing the depths of our lives, not attainable by data alone. As the renowned psychologist (and son of a rabbi) Daniel Kahneman astutely observed, "No one ever made a decision because of a number. They need a story."

Friedman engaged with wit, humor, and one-liners like "You must give people the freedom not to learn from their own experience." He gave me that freedom. Nonetheless, he would want all of us to know that our RO will be known by a focus on strength not pathology, stamina not instant solutions, and responsibility not empathy.

Perhaps more than ever, we need to prepare ourselves for increasing our maturity, which means taking responsibility for our own emotional functioning. As Friedman's mentor Murray Bowen succinctly reminded us, "If you lower anxiety one notch, it's a better world." We all owe thanks to Edwin Friedman for helping us in this process.

PETER L. STEINKE, Ph.D., D.Litt.

ACKNOWLEDGMENTS

Colleagues and friends often asked my father how he found time to be so prolific. Resting his mouth left of center while the corners flirted with a smile, he'd say in his best Murray Bowen Tennessee accent, "Because I have to." Like a shark that must keep moving to survive, this is how my father saw writing.

Edward M. (Ted) Beal's leadership, professional knowledge, editing judgment, and connections were crucial to my father's original manuscript and to this current edition. Of equal importance were his friendship, spirit, and perfectly anointed humor.

Margaret (Peggy) Treadwell's special interest in the connection between emotional process and spirituality bridged my father's coupling of the religious sector with family therapy in both editions. Her introduction of *A Failure of Nerve* to Cynthia Shattuck made this new revised edition of the 1999 private publication possible. Their close collaboration and boundless optimism also kept the project thriving. Susan Luff, Myrna Carpenter, Mickie Crimone, and Gary Emanuel at the Center for Family Process were and continue to be integral in spreading "the word of Ed," as my mother affectionately called it.

Their judicious consultation and unwavering dedication have allowed my father's ideas to proliferate a decade later.

I would especially like to thank Cynthia Shattuck for her vision, enthusiasm, and clear grasp of my father's work. Her brilliant editing, creativity, and playfulness brought new vitality and excitement to this edition.

Special thanks are due also to Susan Kanaan, Jubran Kanaan, Elizabeth Geitz, and Susan Kilborn.

A Failure of Nerve: Leadership in the Age of the Quick Fix could not exist without my mother's commitment and unique insight into my father's thinking. It is to her memory this book is dedicated.

SHIRA FRIEDMAN BOGART

These Acknowledgments were prepared for the 2007 edition of *A Failure of Nerve*.

EDITORS' PREFACE

The premature death of our colleague and friend Edwin H. Friedman on October 31, 1996, illustrates the moral of his fable *The Bridge*: "When things start going really well, watch out." Internationally known as a lecturer and author, Ed's sense of paradox, humor, and particular brand of storytelling were the trademark of his teaching style:

- **"Playfulness can get you out of a rut more successfully than seriousness."**
- **"Triangles are the plaque in the arteries of communication and stress is the effect of our position in the triangle of our families."**
- **"If you are a leader, expect sabotage."**
- **"The colossal misunderstanding of our time is the assumption that insight will work with people who are unmotivated to change. If you want your child, spouse, client, or boss to shape up, stay connected while changing yourself rather than trying to fix them."**

Ed's immediate draw was his paradoxical wit and playfulness, which he always attributed to his mother—"the quickest one-liner I ever met." His ability to capture ambiguities and paradox with a turn of phrase energized and delighted audiences. Those of us who worked with him were challenged in a way that brought hope and courage in defining ourselves, or as Ed entitled his ideas in one sold-out conference, "charting your course in a changing world." When we thanked him, he usually responded, "I'm just the coach: you're the athlete."

Generation to Generation was published in 1985 and provided a new way of thinking about emotional process at home and at work in religious, educational, therapeutic, and business systems. *Friedman's Fables* came out in 1990. By then Ed was deeply engaged with his work on what would become *A Failure of Nerve*, testing it out with students and faculty and incorporating changes raised by questions about leadership as a function of emotional systems. His sudden death was a shock to everyone close to him: many of us had believed that the publication of *A Failure of Nerve* would be the crowning achievement of a remarkable mind and career.

Ed died before completing the second half of his work, in which he planned to challenge the seldom-questioned assumption that human beings function solely according to their nature, gender, or background. Rather, he believed they function according to the position they occupy within the emotional processes of their relationship system, whether family, church, or business. Ed asserted that from the perspective of the emotional process view of reality, the way most leadership programs understand the human phenomenon is tantamount to still assuming that the world is flat.

Ed's widow, Carlyn Friedman, believed *A Failure of Nerve*, even in its unfinished form, was an important part of her husband's legacy, and she was committed to bringing it to the public. She therefore invited us to be the book's principal editors and to make it ready for publication through the Edwin Friedman Trust. As a colleague of Ed's, Ted had already been asked to read the manuscript and offer comments at many points; likewise, as Ed's adjunct faculty member, Peggy knew drafts of various chapters. Yet reading the manuscript in its entirety was particularly exciting because it gave us the opportunity to observe Ed Friedman's mind at work—like seeing an artist's sketch embedded in a partially finished painting. Even though what he envisioned and described was not fully realized, we believed that many readers would appreciate *A Failure of Nerve* as an impetus to free the imagination and stimulate new ways of thinking. Furthermore, the task of actually completing the manuscript became less important to us as we realized, in consultation with Ed's faculty, that while we could edit the syntax, spelling, punctuation, and organization of the text, we could not improve on the original thinking. If we tried to fill in the missing pieces, it would not be Ed's book.

The book was privately published in 1999 under the auspices of the Trust and went into a second printing in 2003. In 2004, while keynoting a conference on congregational leadership in San Diego, Peggy met Cynthia Shattuck, then editorial director at Church Publishing Incorporated. Cynthia expressed interest in bringing it to a wider audience. Ed's children, Shira Bogart and Ari Friedman, were enthusiastic.

Ed was always aware that the original manuscript, even in its unfinished state, needed more work: cutting and polishing, reorganizing, checking historical references, taking out redundancies and duplications, rethinking some shifts and emphases. Throughout the editing process we have stayed faithful to these principles. The original publication consisted of ten chapters written in two parts, but since the final chapters were unfinished, we decided to eliminate this division. The second half of the book is now three chapters in length with a short epilogue, and we have added to them material from the "unfinished chapter notes" originally situated at the end of each chapter. Finally, the copies of ancient maps originally in the first chapter have been removed and we have slightly edited the text to make sure Ed's points are still clear.

As in the original version, even though what he envisioned and described is not fully realized, we believe that "the big picture" does emerge. Ed Friedman's character and wit shine through these pages, continuing to bring his original ideas, fresh insights, and new strategies to light. It has been an honor and privilege to work with Carlyn, Shira, and Ari Friedman so that this important piece of Ed's life-work can reach a larger public on the tenth anniversary of his death.

EDWARD W. (TED) BEAL
M.D. MARGARET M. (PEGGY) TREADWELL, L.I.C.S. W.

This preface was prepared for the 2007 edition of *A Failure of Nerve*.

A FAILURE OF NERVE
IN 52 WEEKS

A YEARLONG LEADERSHIP PLANNER

WEEK ONE
INTRODUCTION

There exists throughout America a rampant sabotaging of leaders who try to stand tall amid the raging anxiety-storms of our time. It is a highly reactive atmosphere pervading all the institutions of our society – a regressive mood that contaminates the decision-making processes of government and corporations at the highest level, and, on the local level, seeps down into the deliberations of neighborhood church, synagogue, hospital, and school boards. It is "something in the air" whose frustrating effect on leaders is the same no matter what their gender, age, or race.

This leadership-toxic climate runs the danger of squandering a natural resource far more vital to the continued evolution of our civilization than any part of the environment. We are polluting our own species. **The more immediate threat to the regeneration—and perhaps even the survival—of American civilization is internal, not external.** It is our tendency to adapt to its immaturity. For whenever a "family" is driven by anxiety, what will also always be present is a failure of nerve among its leaders.

This kind of emotional climate can only be dissipated by clear, decisive, well-defined leadership.

Reflect on your current leadership style. Are you clear and decisive? Or are you not? List the top 3 adjectives you would use to describe your leadership style:

1 _____

_____

2 _____

_____

3 _____

_____

Whenever a "family" (or system) is driven by anxiety, what will also always be present is a failure of nerve among its leaders.

Whether we are considering a family, a work system, or an entire nation, the resistance that sabotages a leader's initiative usually has less to do with the "issue" that ensues than with the fact that the leader took initiative.

This book is about leadership in the land of the quick fix, about leadership in a society so reactive that it cannot choose leaders who might calm its anxiety. It is about the need for clarity and decisiveness in a civilization that inhibits the development of leaders with clarity and decisiveness.

The emphasis here will be on:

- strength, not pathology
- challenge, not comfort
- self-differentiation, not herding for togetherness

This is a difficult perspective to maintain in a "seatbelt society" more oriented toward safety than adventure. This book is not, therefore, for those who prefer peace to progress.

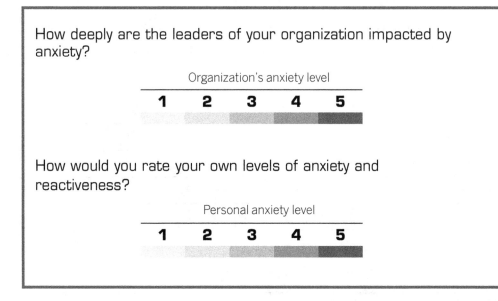

How deeply are the leaders of your organization impacted by anxiety?

Organization's anxiety level

| 1 | 2 | 3 | 4 | 5 |

How would you rate your own levels of anxiety and reactiveness?

Personal anxiety level

| 1 | 2 | 3 | 4 | 5 |

Leadership in America is stuck in the rut of trying harder and harder without obtaining significantly new results. The rut runs deep, affecting all the institutions of our society irrespective of size or purpose. It affects even those institutions that try to tackle the problem: universities, thinktanks, and consultants. These institutions are "stuck," and there exists a connection between the paralysis that leaders experience and the paralysis in the thinking processes of those who would get them unstuck.

What results drive you and your organization? What are the barriers you perceive are keeping you from achieving those results?

_____

_____

_____

_____

_____

_____

_____

Consider the year ahead. What do you need to accomplish? Don't lose your nerve! Work to keep others from diverting your purpose.

_____

_____

_____

_____

_____

_____

_____

Thought for the week:
«When anxiety reaches certain thresholds,
even the most learned ideas can begin
to function as superstitions.»

MONDAY _____ / _____

TUESDAY _____ / _____

WEDNESDAY _____ / _____

THURSDAY _____ / _____

FRIDAY _____ / _____

WEEKEND _____ / _____

WEEK TWO
SELF-DIFFERENTIATED LEADERS

While each branch of American society thought its troubles were due to something within its own discipline, or were particular to its own region, the problems were, as I had already begun to suspect, nationwide.

Here are four major similarities in the thinking and functioning of America's families and institutions that I have observed everywhere.

Check any that you have observed at work in the leadership of your organization:

❏ **A regressive, counter-evolutionary trend** in which the most dependent members of any organization set the agendas and where adaptation is toward weakness rather than strength, leveraging power to the most anxious members, rather than toward the energetic, the visionary, the imaginative.

❏ **A devaluation of the process of individuation** so that leaders tend to rely more on expertise than on their own capacity to be decisive.

❏ **An obsession with data and technique** that has become a form of addiction. Decision makers avoid or deny the very emotional processes within their institutions that might contribute to their institution's "persistence in form."

❏ **A widespread misunderstanding about the relational nature of destructive processes in institutions** that leads leaders to assume toxic forces can be regulated through reasonableness, love, and striving for consensus. It prevents them from setting limits to the invasiveness of those who lack self-regulation.

This book will encourage leaders to focus **first on their own integrity and on the nature of their own presence** rather than on techniques for manipulating or motivating others. Leadership is essentially an emotional process rather than a cognitive phenomenon.

A well-differentiated leader:

WORD MATRIX

Is Not	Is
Autocratic	Non-anxious
Obsessed with data	Sometimes challenging
Reliant on consultants	In control of their own reactivity

Looking at the lists above, do you identify most strongly with the attributes in the left column, or the right? What is one step you can take today to expand your capacity for well-differentiated leadership?

_____

_____

_____

_____

_____

_____

A well-differentiated leader has clarity about his or her life goals and, therefore, is less likely to become lost in the anxious emotional processes swirling about. **They can remain separate while still remaining connected.** No one does this easily, but most leaders can improve their capacity.

There is sometimes a confusion of self with selfishness. The tension of the self and togetherness is universal. It appears in areas as diverse as biology, marriage, and politics. There is a tilt toward the togetherness end of the scale, however, when a relationship system becomes emotionally regressed. Then, self becomes threatening to the togetherness needs of the group and is perceived as cruel, cold, selfish.

The way out of this dilemma is not by finding the proper balance of self and togetherness, but by reorienting one's understanding of togetherness and self so they are made continuous rather than polarized.

Sometimes you must put your own needs first for the good of others. Describe a time that you or someone you know acted "selfishly," for the betterment of those around them, whether for their workplace, family, or other community group:

_____

_____

_____

_____

Leadership is essentially an emotional process rather than a *cognitive* phenomenon. Self-differentiation is not anti-togetherness; on the contrary, it is a force that modifies the emotional processes within any group's togetherness so that a leader actually promotes community through the emerging self-differentiation (autonomy, independence, individuality) of the other members.

SELF-ASSESSMENT

I make decisions based on my own vision, not the desires of others.

○ **TRUE**　○ **FALSE**

Thought for the week:
«Chronic criticism is often a sign that the
leader is functioning better.»

MONDAY _____ / _____

....
....
....
....
....
....

TUESDAY _____ / _____

....
....
....
....
....
....

WEDNESDAY _____ / _____

....
....
....
....
....
....

THURSDAY _____ / _____

....
....
....
....
....
....

FRIDAY _____ / _____

....
....
....
....
....
....

WEEKEND _____ / _____

....
....
....
....
....
....

WEEK THREE
IMAGINATIVE GRIDLOCK

Late fifteenth-century Europe was living in the wake of the plagues, the breakdown of the feudal order, and the inability of an often corrupt church to ring true. There had not been a major scientific discovery for a thousand years. There had not been a major scientific journey for a thousand years.

Then, as if suddenly, the depression lifts like a morning mist, and the Renaissance that had been germinating sprouts vigorously. **The imaginative gridlock that had largely beclouded Europe's inventiveness for more than a millennium dissolves forever.** Over the next half century, more radical change occurred in every field of human endeavor than had ever happened before, or since.

Underlying all this was a basic, all-embracing change. The two worldviews by which European civilization had oriented itself were turned on their heads:

- **The view that the land mass on our planet was situated entirely above the equator, extending contiguously from western Europe to eastern Asia.**
- **The notion that the other planets and stars revolved around the earth, which was situated at the center of the universe.**

In an imaginatively gridlocked system, more learning will not, on its own, automatically change the way people see things. There must first be a shift in the emotional processes of that institution. To imagine the unimaginable, people must be able to separate themselves from the emotional processes that surround them. Without this understanding, it becomes impossible to realize how our learning can prevent us from learning more.

SELF-ASSESSMENT

I live in a time of imaginative gridlock.

○ **TRUE**   ○ **FALSE**

There are three major, interlocking characteristics common to any relationship system that has become imaginatively gridlocked:

- **an unending treadmill of trying harder**
- **looking for answers rather than reframing questions**
- **either/or thinking that creates false dichotomies**

These attributes are both symptom and cause of a locked-in perspective. All three describe any similarly stuck relationship system at any time, be it a marriage, a family, an organization, or a nation. And all three attributes, while appearing to be cognitive, are symptomatic of surrounding emotional processes.

Trying Harder
This treadmill effect of trying harder is well known to marriage partners who keep trying to change their partners, managers who keep trying harder to change those they manage, CEOs who keep trying harder to change their managers, consultants who keep trying harder to change CEOs, and social scientists who keep trying harder to explain what is happening.

The treadmill of trying harder is driven by the assumption that failure is due to the fact that one did not try hard enough, use the right technique, or get enough information. This assumption overlooks the possibility that thinking processes themselves are stuck and imagination gridlocked because of emotional processes within the wider relationship system.

Are there areas of your life or work that never seem to improve in proportion with the effort you put into them? Choose one, then take a step back. Beyond data and logic, what underlying emotions or emotional processes are at play?

_____

_____

_____

Answers Rather Than Questions
The second attribute of imaginatively gridlocked relationship systems is a continual search for new answers to old questions rather than an effort to reframe the questions themselves. **In the search for the solution to any problem, questions are always more important than answers** because the way one frames the question, or the problem, predetermines the range of answers one can receive in response. Seeking answers can be its own treadmill. Changing the question enables one to step off.

SELF-ASSESSMENT

Effort is more important than creativity of thought.

○ **TRUE**   ○ **FALSE**

Either/Or Thinking
The third characteristic of gridlocked relationship systems is either/or, black-or-white, all-or-nothing ways of thinking that restrict the options of the mind. Intense polarizations are symptomatic of underlying emotional processes rather than the subject matter of the polarizing issue. **Rigid dichotomies almost always hint that there is something wrong in the original orientation.**

The great either/or question in Columbus's time was: Is it three thousand or ten thousand miles from Europe to Japan? With hindsight, it is hard for us to conceive that neither side could imagine a third possibility: another piece of land in between.

Consider an issue that strongly divides you and a colleague or partner. Putting your emotional attachment to your current convictions aside, is there another solution neither of you has considered? What would it entail?

_____

_____

_____

_____

Thought for the week:
«When troubled couples make a breakthrough, often the issues that they differed over are not resolved, but they both have become less reactive to the differences.»

MONDAY _____ / _____

TUESDAY _____ / _____

WEDNESDAY _____ / _____

THURSDAY _____ / _____

FRIDAY _____ / _____

WEEKEND _____ / _____

WEEK FOUR
THE SPIRIT OF ADVENTURE

The process of discovery that freed Europe from its imaginative gridlock of a thousand years is in large part about the relationship between risk and reality—which means it is also basically about leadership. It teaches the vital importance of leadership if a relationship system is to undergo a fundamental reorientation.

Conditions must be propitious for imagination boldness, or energy to bear fruit; but **for ripe times to benefit from what they have to offer, someone simply must be able to separate himself or herself enough from surrounding emotional processes to go first.**

Leaders who embody the spirit of adventure must at certain times prioritize discovery over the safety of the status quo. Where would you place your current focus on the scale below?

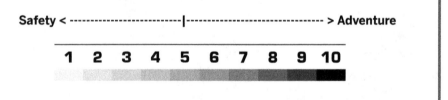

Safety < --------------------------|-------------------------- > Adventure

1   2   3   4   5   6   7   8   9   10

Many have pointed to the relationship between risk and imagination and observed that it is safer to confine one's thoughts to the conventional. In the process of reorientation, however, the connection is far more fundamental. There is a relationship between risk and reality that involves not risk and one's sense of reality, which is a psychological concept, but nerve and reality itself. **If imagination involves risk, the willingness to risk is critical to validating one's perceptions.**

Three facets of the discovery process convey this relationship between risk and reality.

- when the quest is driven by adventure rather than certainty, mistakes are not ultimately important
- serendipity is important in freeing oneself from one's own thinking processes
- overcoming imaginative barriers is an act of will

The Freedom to Make Mistakes

To say that mistakes are unimportant may overstate the case. Yet Europe's reorientation process clearly demonstrates that even though huge errors were made along the way—there were maps with islands in the Atlantic, tigers in the Appalachians, and whole host of other demons, beasties, and cannibals decorating the cartography of the day—they turned out to be a small price to pay for getting the ships out of the harbor.

Sometimes the cartographers seem to have had more power to determine reality than the explorers themselves. Yet the system as a whole worked in the Age of Exploration because the all-encompassing, surrounding emotional atmosphere was conducive to **excitement and adventure rather than the failure of nerve** that always accompanies anxiety and a quest for certainty.

Our current age of discovery is very different.

How does your current organization handle mistakes? Describe a time when you a took a risk and it didn't pay off. What did you learn from that experience?

_____

_____

_____

_____

_____

_____

The Value of Chance

If making mistakes is relatively unimportant in an atmosphere of adventure, willingness to encounter serendipity is vital to its continuing spirit. Throughout the Age of Exploration, trips are beset by the unforeseen. The great lesson here for all imaginatively gridlocked systems is that **the acceptance and even cherishing of uncertainty is critical to keeping the human mind from voyaging into the delusion of omniscience**. The willingness to encounter serendipity is the best antidote we have for the arrogance of thinking we know.

SELF-ASSESSMENT

Superior leaderships stems from superior knowledge.

○ **TRUE** ○ **FALSE**

Exposing oneself to chance is often the only way to provide the kind of mind-jarring experience of novelty that can make us realize that what we thought was reality was only a mirror of our minds.

The willingness to encounter the unexpected enables us to imagine the unimaginable. No society can continue to evolve as long as it makes cloistered virtues supreme.

Has a mistake or unexpected outcome ever led you to pursue a new path? Were you initially tempted to write off the experience as a failure?

_____

_____

_____

How can you keep your mind open to chance opportunities in the future?

_____

_____

_____

Thought for the week:
«Contemporary American civilization is as misoriented
about the environment of relationships as the medieval
world was misoriented about the Earth and the sky.»

MONDAY _____ / _____

TUESDAY _____ / _____

WEDNESDAY _____ / _____

THURSDAY _____ / _____

FRIDAY _____ / _____

WEEKEND _____ / _____

WEEK FIVE
EMOTIONAL BARRIERS

The belief that the equator defined the end of the world limited the spirit necessary to produce reality. The equator served as an emotional barrier, a belief born of mythology and kept in place by anxiety. Such beliefs take hold to the extent that society is driven by anxiety rather than adventure. I have called them *imaginative* or *emotional barriers* rather than simply myths because their effect is more than cerebral. Their influence spreads throughout society well beyond the content of their subject. When these barriers are broken, more change occurs than could have been attributed to the specific content of the basic myth.

The attempt to run a mile in less than four minutes serves as an excellent illustration of the power such emotional barriers can have. Sports pages would actually ask whether it was physically possible for a man to run a mile faster than four minutes. The four-minute mile took on the character of a constant, like the speed of light, a natural barrier. But when Roger Bannister finally broke that barrier in 1957, the following year three men broke it in the same race.

Many organizations tacitly accept beliefs or assumptions that deserve to be questioned. List two or three assumptions within your immediate team or larger organization that you would like to re-evaluate.

1._____

_____

2._____

_____

3._____

_____

The power of emotional barriers to restrict both the imaginative capacity and the adventure necessary for freeing the imagination is evidenced by what followed so quickly in the wake of the historic crossing of the equator. Within half a century Magellan's circumnavigation had radically altered the fifteen-hundred-year-old Ptolemaic view of the entire planet. Less than twenty years after that, Copernicus irrevocably changed Ptolemy's generally accepted view of the cosmos.

Have you set any "natural limits" on yourself? List three things you have always assumed you cannot do or wouldn't be good at.

1. _____

2. _____

3. _____

Choose one limit, then write out a plan for altering the outcome. Assuming that you can do it, how might you go about it?

_____

_____

_____

_____

We will return to the theme of breaking barriers later. For now, keep in mind these three mind-sets (or, better, emotional-sets) that limit the horizons of leaders today. They are generally accepted fallacies about:

- *Data*: that data are more vital to leadership than the capacity to be decisive
- *Empathy*: that feeling for others helps them mature or become more responsible
- *Self*: that selfishness is a greater danger to a community than the loss of integrity that comes from having no self

To overcome our culture of anxiety and become bold, self-differentiated leaders, we must first reorient our conception of leadership away from "old world" definitions and embrace the new. From the columns below, select the definition that represents a "new world" leader.

WORD MATRIX

Imagination is cerebral	Imagination is emotional
Anxiety is in the mind	Anxiety is between people
The capacity to be decisive is more important than knowing everything	Leaders should be as informed as possible
A leader's "selfishness" destroys community	A leader's self is essential to the integrity of a new community
Leaders should foster responsibility for one's own being and destiny	Leaders should foster feelings and sensitivity
Criticism and sabotage are dangers to be avoided	Criticism can be a sign of success; preserve self and stay connected

Leaders should strive to overcome their emotional barriers, open themselves up to chance, and never let the fear of failure keep them from pursuing an opportunity. With this in mind, set yourself one long-term goal. Name one area of your organization that you will (ad)venture into in the coming year. Goal:

_____

_____

_____

Thought for the week:
«Emotional barriers act as a plaque in the arteries of communication and perception; they stop up the entire artery, not just the location at which they are found.»

MONDAY _____ / _____

_____
_____
_____
_____
_____

TUESDAY _____ / _____

_____
_____
_____
_____
_____

WEDNESDAY _____ / _____

_____
_____
_____
_____
_____

THURSDAY _____ / _____

_____
_____
_____
_____
_____

FRIDAY _____ / _____

_____
_____
_____
_____
_____

WEEKEND _____ / _____

_____
_____
_____
_____
_____

WEEK SIX
THE COUNTER-EVOLUTIONARY AGE

There are some curious similarities between the anxious emotional process of late-fifteenth-century medieval Europe and late-twentieth-century America that help highlight the factors that are toxic to leadership in our time. Each age:

- has been destabilized by the breakdown of institutions around which society organized itself
- is characterized by radical power shifts in traditional alliances
- is affected by a global economy that makes old, reliable rules irrelevant or inoperative
- is impacted by a radical new technology that intensifies the connections of society's members

There are similarities in the regressive symptoms that can result when anxiety becomes chronic. **Both periods share what I call a tendency towards societal regression.**

Whereas medieval Europe's lack of cohesion enabled individuals to separate themselves from its regressive emotional climate, our technology keeps us in simultaneous touch with one another, making it difficult not to become caught up in the surrounding system anxiety. This enmeshment inhibits the individuation that is the essential precondition for bold leadership and imaginative thinking.

SELF-ASSESSMENTS

I find it easy to distance myself from current trends in societal thinking.

○ **TRUE**   ○ **FALSE**

I focus on my own emotions before the emotional reactions of others.

○ **TRUE**   ○ **FALSE**

Regressive processes are pervasive throughout American civilization today in families, in institutions, and in society at large. It is the automatic and reciprocal feedback among these three emotional fields that makes society's anxiety systemic.

America has become so chronically anxious that our society has gone into an age of emotional regression that is toxic to well-defined leadership. This regression is characterized principally by a devaluing and denigration of the well-differentiated self.

In contrast to the Renaissance spirit of adventure, American civilization has instead been shaped into an illusive and often compulsive search for safety and certainty.

Safety is typically considered a positive goal. Why then might safety be a dangerous guiding principle for a leader?

_____

_____

_____

_____

Five characteristics of chronically anxious families manifest throughout the greater American family today. I will demonstrate their regressive effects on our thinking about and the function, formation, and expression of leadership, among parents and presidents. Those five characteristics are:

1. Reactivity
2. Herding
3. Blame displacement
4. A quick-fix mentality
5. Lack of well-differentiated leadership

To reorient oneself away from a focus on technology toward a focus on emotional processes requires that we think in ways that are not only different from traditional routes but that also sometimes go in the opposite direction. Chief among the evolutionary principles of life that have been basic to the development of our species are the following:

- self-regulation of instinctual drive
- adaptation to strength rather than weakness
- a growth-producing response to challenge
- allowing time for maturing processes to evolve
- the preservation of individuality and integrity

While society progresses technologically, it may be regressing in other ways. Does your organization preserve the principles of life listed above? Underline any principle you believe is regressing. What have you observed?

_____

_____

_____

_____

_____

_____

_____

_____

Societal regression is about the perversion of progress into a counter-evolutionary mode. In a societal regression, these evolutionary principles of life become distorted, perverted, or actually reversed. When a society or institution is in a state of emotional regression, it will put its technological advances to the service of its regression, so that the more it advances on one level, the more it regresses on another.

Thought for the week:
«In any society, chronic anxiety can induce an approach to life that is counter-evolutionary: one does not need dictators in order to create a totalitarian society.»

MONDAY _____ / _____ | **TUESDAY** _____ / _____

....
....
....
....
....

WEDNESDAY _____ / _____ | **THURSDAY** _____ / _____

....
....
....
....

FRIDAY _____ / _____ | **WEEKEND** _____ / _____

....
....
....
....

WEEK SEVEN
EMOTIONAL REGRESSION

Emotional regression is more of a "going down" than a "going back"; it is a devolution rather than evolution. It has to do with a lowering of maturity, rather than a reduction in the gross national product. At the same time that a society is "pro-gressing" technologically it can be "re-gressing" emotionally. It will put its technological advances to the service of its regression, so that the more it advances on one level the more it regresses on another.

The ultimate irony of societal regression is that eventually it co-opts the very institutions that train and support the leaders who could pull a society out of its devolution. It does this by concentrating their focus on data and technique rather than on emotional process and the leader's own self. The focus on data and technique is itself a characteristic of emotional regression; namely, avoidance or denial of the fact that it is happening.

SELF-ASSESSMENTS

Emotional regression results in the erosion of the individuation necessary for well-defined leadership to arise.

○ TRUE   ○ FALSE

In the shaping of any institution, emotional processes are more powerful than the nature of its structure or makeup.

○ TRUE   ○ FALSE

The concept of an emotionally regressed society was first developed by Dr. Murray Bowen. One of the seminal thinkers in the relatively new field of family therapy, Bowen had begun to apply his observations of deeply disturbed families to society itself. Bowen focused on the underlying natural systems principles that all families share, even though they might express those universal principles in different cultural garb.

The most critical issues in understanding human institutions are not their customs, rituals, and ceremonies, but rather:

❏ How well human institutions handle the tension between individuality and togetherness
❏ Their ability to maintain their integrity during crisis
❏ Their capacity to produce well-differentiated leadership

One cannot say, after all, that the families of any given ethnicity or even class are more mature than those of another background. It is rather the multigenerational emotional process, transmitted from generation to generation uniquely by each family, that puts aspects of its cultural or ethnic background to its own emotional service.

Have you inherited any emotional processing from your own family, or from previous employers? How about your company at large—perhaps from a merger or acquisition? How do these emotional processes impact your ability (or your company's ability) to maintain integrity during a crisis?

_____

_____

_____

_____

_____

_____

_____

_____

Bowen was struck by the similarities between what he had been observing with increasing frequency in American society everywhere and what he had been used to seeing in chronically anxious families. He went on to develop the idea that, as with families, the anxiety curve of an entire civilization goes through periods when it rises or falls. An entire society could lose its ability to cope with change when certain factors occur simultaneously:

❑ Anxiety escalates as a society is overwhelmed by the quantity and speed of change

❑ The institutions that traditionally absorb or bind off society's anxiety are no longer able to absorb it

When both of these factors occur at the same time, the societal leaders lose their capacity to lead. Their response to challenge becomes narrow and loses resiliency and their overall imaginative capacity becomes stuck. They soon find themselves on a treadmill of efforts to get free.

Describe how you typically react to change. Are you fearful of new processes, or eager to embrace them? Have you ever lost out as a result of a hesitancy to embrace change?

_____

_____

_____

_____

_____

_____

_____

_____

_____

Thought for the week:
«Key variables have less to do with institutions'
respective cultural traditions than with the way their
members are connected emotionally.»

MONDAY ____ / ____

TUESDAY ____ / ____

WEDNESDAY ____ / ____

THURSDAY ____ / ____

FRIDAY ____ / ____

WEEKEND ____ / ____

WEEK EIGHT
THE SPECTER OF CHRONIC ANXIETY

Chronic anxiety is systemic; it is deeper and more embracing than community nervousness. Rather than something that resides within the psyche of each one, it is something that can envelop, if not actually connect, people. Its expression is not dependent on time or events, though specific happenings could seem to trigger it.

The issues over which chronically anxious systems become concerned, therefore, are more likely to be the focus of their anxiety rather than its cause. Yet assuming that what a family or institution is worried about is what is "causing" its anxiety is tantamount to blaming a blown-away house for attracting the tornado that uprooted it.

When an entire society stays focused on the acute symptoms of its chronic anxiety—violence, drugs, crime, economic factors, and so on—rather than the emotional processes that keep them chronic, they will recycle their problems perpetually.

List three symptoms of disfunction within your organization on the left. What might be the underlying emotional process causing the symptoms? List your answer on the right.

Symptom	Cause
1.	1.
2.	2.
3.	3.

The more chronic anxiety becomes systemic in any institution, the more likely that relationship system is to stay oriented toward its symptoms. **There is no way out of a chronic condition unless one is willing to go through an acute, temporarily more painful, phase.**

Whether we are considering a toothache, a tumor, or a relational problem, most individuals and most social systems will revert to chronic conditions of bearable pain rather than face the temporarily more intense anguish of acute conditions that are the gateway to becoming free.

On a scale of 1-5, rate yourself on each of the statements below:

I am focused on identifying the source of problems, not symptoms.

I have distanced myself from the chronic anxiety in my organization.

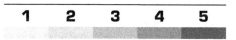

I am prepared to face uncomfortable challenges.

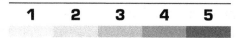

There are five interlocking characteristics of chronically anxious institutions, with regressive parallels in the greater American family of today. Each is regressive because it subverts a major principle of the way life on this planet has survived and evolved.

SELF-ASSESSMENT

Test yourself: What are the five characteristics of chronically anxious systems, first discussed in Week Six?

1. R_____

2. H_____

3. B_____

4. Q_____

5. F _____

All five characteristics contribute to one another, although the fifth may be the link among them all. All families or institutions will at times exhibit these characteristics when their anxiety reaches certain thresholds, and probably no family or institution is more than 70 percent free of them over any extended period of time.

According to E. O. Wilson, the three essential characteristics for an enduring society are cooperation, cohesiveness, and altruism. **In civilized human societies these characteristics have been made possible by the development of our ability to regulate our instincts rather than let them drive us automatically.** Under conditions of chronic anxiety, however, that capacity is eroded—and with it go cooperation, cohesiveness, and altruism.

Thought for the week:
«Chronic conditions, precisely because they are more bearable, also tend to be more withering over time.»

MONDAY _____ / _____

TUESDAY _____ / _____

WEDNESDAY _____ / _____

THURSDAY _____ / _____

FRIDAY _____ / _____

WEEKEND _____ / _____

WEEK NINE

CHARACTERISTICS OF THE CHRONICALLY ANXIOUS

CHARACTERISTIC ONE: REACTIVITY

The most blatant characteristic of chronically anxious systems is the vicious cycle of intense *reactivity* of each member to events and to one another. Responses in chronically anxious systems tend to be triggered by outside stimuli rather than from within. Communication is marked more by diagnostic or labelling "you" positions rather than by self-defining "I" statements. Members are constantly making things more "personal."

In such systems, members wind up focused on the latest, most immediate crisis, and remain incapable of gaining the distance that would enable them to see the emotional processes in which they are engulfed. They will stay fixed on symptoms, rather than on the emotional processes that are driving those matters to become "issues."

In order to break out of anxious conversation cycles, leaders must focus on their own convictions, rather than on the emotions of others.

Reactive: "You just don't get it…"
Calm: "Here is how I perceive it…"

Imagine you are having a conversation with a colleague who disagrees with a proposal you have made. Practice developing self-defining ways to communicate your view:

"I _____

_____ "

"I _____

_____ "

What also contributes to this loss of perspective is the disappearance of playfulness, which is an ingredient in both intimacy and the ability to maintain distance. The relationship between anxiety and seriousness is so predictable that the absence of playfulness in any institution is almost always a clue to the degree of its emotional regression.

But **the most damaging effect of intense reactivity in any family or organization is on its capacity to produce or support a leader**. As the capacity of any member to achieve self-regulation or distance disintegrates, so does the ability, or desire, to lead. Reactivity, therefore, eventually makes chronically anxious organizations leaderless, either by:

❏ Preventing potential leaders from emerging
❏ Wearing down leaders by sabotaging their initiatives and resolve

As with any chronically anxious family, there is in American society today an intense quickness to interfere in another's self-expression, to overreact to any perceived hurt, to take all disagreement too seriously, and to brand the opposition with ad hominem personal epithets. This hardens hearts and leaves little room for forgiveness or balanced accommodation.

The reactivity that is characteristic of emotionally regressed America today can induce a "dis-courag-ing" failure of nerve among society's most individualistic leaders.

Many leaders are enervated by the cycle of reactivity that permeates their organization. Repeating a personal mantra can be an effective tool for rebuilding your courage and refreshing your spirits. In the space below, try crafting a mantra or personal statement:

_____

_____

_____

_____

CHARACTERISTIC TWO: THE HERD INSTINCT

A critical principle of evolution has been that as new forms develop, life evolves in the direction of its strengths by preserving a balance between togetherness and individuality. The herding instinct in a chronically anxious system upsets that balance, however, by encouraging the force for togetherness to smother the force for individuality.

A major byproduct of reactivity is the dominance of the forces for togetherness. This emotional herding reinforces many of the factors regarding the loss of space and distance. When chronic anxiety reaches systemic proportions, the desire for good feelings rather than progress will on its own promote togetherness over individuality. The "togetherness" that forms under such circumstances is undifferentiated. The chronically anxious, herding organization seems to develop a "self" of its own to which everyone is expected to adapt, and they will be far more willing to risk losing its leadership than to lose those who disturb their togetherness with their immature responses.

Below are several symptoms of a system with a herding mentality. Check any that you have observed at work in your organization:

- Peace is valued over progress
- Feelings are valued over ideas
- Comfort is valued over novelty
- Either/or mindset dominates problem-solving

The major effect of this system on leadership is that it hinders the capacity to be decisive. Herding erodes the sense of self. And the less confidence leaders have in their ability to stand alone after they make a decision, the less likely they are to make one.

Thought for the week:
«A good rule of thumb for leaders is that when people start calling them names there is a good chance they are going in the right direction.»

MONDAY _____ / _____

TUESDAY _____ / _____

WEDNESDAY _____ / _____

THURSDAY _____ / _____

FRIDAY _____ / _____

WEEKEND _____ / _____

WEEK TEN
MORE CHARACTERISTICS OF THE CHRONICALLY ANXIOUS

CHARACTERISTIC THREE: BLAME DISPLACEMENT

Chronically anxious families encourage blame rather than ownership. This is a natural by-product of the erosion of the well-differentiated self that results from a herding attitude. The capacity to take responsibility for one's own being and destiny requires integrity. The same avoidance of looking inward that leads members to cast blame outside the family also prevents family members from looking inward for the support of their own natural resources. The focus is constantly on pathology rather than strength, since it protects us from the far more difficult task of personal responsibility.

More mature families or organizations that focus primarily on their own response to trauma generally heal faster. They sometimes even grow—that is, evolve—to a higher capacity for dealing with trauma as a result of their encounter with challenge. This is how the self of any human being grows—by broadening the repertoire of its responses.

WORD MATRIX

The concept of leadership is totally incompatible with displacing blame. From the columns below, circle the symptoms of blame displacement in a regressive organization.

Loss of integrity and accountability	Willing to take risks for the greater good
Cynical pessimism	Quick to assign blame
Focus on safety	Recognizes fault within the system

CHARACTERISTIC FOUR: THE QUICK-FIX MENTALITY

Life processes evolve by taking their time. Growth, whether of a flower or of a baby, follows similar laws to this day, and growth, meaning maturation, evolves in the same way. But the chronically anxious system is impatient; escapist thinking leads it to assume that problems can be fixed in a linear way. The quick-fix mentality is the other side of the coin of displacement. Both are a flight from challenge, simplistic in their conception of life, and outwardly focused. Both avoid dealing with the emotional processes that devalue the self. **Ultimately, both depreciate the integrity of the leader**.

What makes the chronically anxious system's anxiety chronic is not its pain, but the way it deals with its pain. The root word for anxiety means pain, as in anguish or angst. Members of a chronically anxious organization will seek those professionals who will help them avoid or reduce their pain as quickly as possible, not those who would encourage them to endure their pain in order to move steadfastly toward higher goals. Focused always on symptom relief rather than on fundamental change in emotional processes that underlie their symptoms, they will constantly seek saviors, then pressure the expert for magical solutions.

When leaders cater to the demand for a quick fix, rather than encouraging those in their system to deal with their own emotional being, these leaders miss out on challenging opportunities to grow. Have you ever rushed to "solve" a problem too quickly just to make others happy? What systemic problems did this force you overlook or ignore? How might you tackle the problem now?

_____

_____

_____

_____

_____

CHARACTERISTIC FIVE: POORLY DIFFERENTIATED LEADERSHIP

The four major characteristics of chronically anxious systems conspire to produce the fifth: the lack of well-differentiated leadership. Chronically anxious organizations always lack a well-differentiated leader who can maintain a non-anxious, well-principled presence and stay outside of the organizations' reactive, quick-fix processes to sufficiently take stands.

The major regressive effects on leadership of chronic anxiety both in personal families and in the greater American family are these:

- **Leaders lack the distance to think out their vision clearly**
- **Leaders are led hither and yon by crisis after crisis**
- **Leaders are reluctant to take well-defined stands**
- **Leaders are selected who lack the maturity and sense of self to deal with sabotage**

These are in stark contrast to the major principles of leadership characteristic of the Renaissance explorers:

- **The capacity to separate oneself from surrounding emotional processes (/ 5)**
- **The capacity to obtain clarity about one's principles and visions (/ 5)**
- **The willingness to be exposed and to be vulnerable (/ 5)**
- **Persistence in the face of inertial resistance (/ 5)**
- **Self-regulation in the face of reactive sabotage (/ 5)**

Rate yourself against the five principles of well-differentiated leadership above. Reflect on the characteristic that offers the most opportunity for growth. How might you work to strengthen that characteristic within yourself?

_____

_____

_____

Thought for the week:
«If one allows a sand pile to build up, grain by grain, at some point one more grain will cause an avalanche.»

MONDAY ____ / ____

....
....
....
....
....

TUESDAY ____ / ____

....
....
....
....
....

WEDNESDAY ____ / ____

....
....
....
....
....

THURSDAY ____ / ____

....
....
....
....
....

FRIDAY ____ / ____

....
....
....
....
....

WEEKEND ____ / ____

....
....
....
....
....

WEEK ELEVEN
THE FALLACY OF EXPERTISE

If you went back in history two thousand years, the amount of information that then existed would fit in a single library or two. Today, the quantity of data that is available to leaders is so huge as to be unimaginable. Indeed, with present computer technology, every time a new bit of information is conceived, it has the potential immediately to cross-pollinate with existing data and to double—and that is happening in a myriad of situations every nanosecond. Data today expand at a proportion so much greater than time passes that the expansion is becoming a quantum phenomenon. Now instead of going back two thousand years, suppose you were to project forward two thousand years. How much data will there be?

What I am driving at is this: **As long as leaders base their confidence on how much data they have acquired, they are doomed to feeling inadequate, forever**. They will never catch up. Yet everywhere in our society, the social science construction of reality has confused information with expertise, know-how with wisdom, change with almost anything new, and complexity with profundity. The data deluge can only be harnessed when leaders recognize that not all information is worth gathering and develop criteria for discerning what information is important to leadership.

What are your go-to sources for information? Who do you consult when making a decision? Write out a list below. Are all of the sources you've provided necessary, or do some keep you from acting in a decisive and timely manner?

_____

_____

_____

_____

_____

The great myth of our data-gathering era that affects leaders, parents, and healers alike has two sides: "If only we knew enough, we could do (or fix) anything," and its obverse, "If we failed it is because we did not use the right method." This fallacy orients leaders toward "know-how" rather than the nature of their own being.

A further consequence of our orientation toward data and technique rather than toward emotional process devalues the self in several related ways that affect leadership:

- It overwhelms leaders
- It confuses leaders with contradictory results
- It emphasizes weakness rather than strength
- It "de-selfs" leaders by ignoring the variable of individuation

This data deluge affects all members of society and erodes the confidence, judgement, and decisiveness of leaders in particular. Despite its anxiety provoking effects, the proliferation of data also has an addictive quality. Leaders "imbibe" data as a way of dealing with their own chronic anxiety.

SELF-ASSESSMENTS

I have read and understood every important document in my field.

○ **TRUE**   ○ **FALSE**

I believe that using data can eliminate risk from decision making.

○ **TRUE**   ○ **FALSE**

I feel paralyzed when asked to make a choice without first consulting multiple sources.

○ **TRUE**   ○ **FALSE**

The latest understanding of the nature of the human brain has out-distanced the "old world" knowledge on which most contemporary leadership theory is based. And it is precisely the "old world" focus on data and technique rather than emotional process that contributes to that fundamental understanding. We now know that data and emotional process are integrated at the most fundamental levels of brain functioning. This has revolutionary consequences for leadership; **in any age, models of leadership must square with the latest understanding of the connection between the brain and the body**.

Conventional models of the brain that separate out the brain's cognitive functioning from our broader emotional heritage—that which connects us with the universal natural processes that govern all life on this planet—is, ironically, in danger of subverting the brain into a counter-evolutionary force. To the extent that the variables of emotional processes are omitted in any family or organizational data gathering activity—and the more successful the human brain becomes in its endeavors to produce more "knowledge"—the more stuck the human animal will become in the knowledge it produces.

This brings us back to the three characteristics of an imaginatively gridlocked society:

- A treadmill of always trying harder
- A focus on finding answers rather than reframing questions
- A polarization into false dichotomies

While it is important for leaders to remain informed, an overreliance on data can create a lack of confidence in one's instincts and abilities. Reflect on your own decision-making and data-gathering processes. Are they out of balance? Do you have trust in your own experience and expertise?

_____

_____

_____

_____

Thought for the week:
«The amount of responsibility one takes for his or her own life is the quintessential issue of leadership and self.»

MONDAY _____ / _____

....
....
....
....
....

TUESDAY _____ / _____

....
....
....
....
....

WEDNESDAY _____ / _____

....
....
....
....
....

THURSDAY _____ / _____

....
....
....
....
....

FRIDAY _____ / _____

....
....
....
....
....

WEEKEND _____ / _____

....
....
....
....
....

WEEK TWELVE
DATA AND LEADERSHIP IN MEDICINE

By 1990, the number of indexed articles that a physician could refer to had reached six hundred thousand. If a physician were to read two articles a day for twelve months, at the end of the year **the physician would be eight hundred years further behind than when he started**. The focus on data continues throughout the physicians life, and has a significant effect not only on how the healer practices but also on the response of patients to their condition.

The proliferation of data (and the denial of emotional processes) begins with the well-known intake forms and goes further on standardized insurance forms, which list more disease syndromes than one could have ever thought possible. It cannot be that whoever or whatever organized this universe set it up in such a way that this much information would be necessary in order to function effectively.

Staying abreast of new data in any given field has become a Sisyphean task. What does this mean for so-called "experts" in their fields? What do you think truly sets them apart from their peers?

_____

_____

_____

_____

_____

_____

_____

Such refinement of data can have a significant impact on both doctor and patient. The data deluge can distract physicians from focusing on their own healing power. This includes not only their overall objectivity and diagnostic astuteness but also their capacity to regulate their own anxiety with regard to both their patients' and their attorney's anxieties. How a physician manages their anxiety can be a vital component in a patient's recovery.

SELF-ASSESSMENT

I am easily overwhelmed or distracted by data

○ TRUE   ○ FALSE

Nowhere on the ubiquitous medical intake forms are questions that would inform the physician of a given patient's capacity for recuperation, questions that might by their very asking challenge patients to be more responsible for their own condition. The omission of the patient's own response on forms and in statistics gives the data a morbidly deterministic quality and puts the patient into an emotional bind.

Once one begins to include emotional variables in the overall data—such as emotional binds, past tendencies in crisis, and the capacity to maintain resolve—it becomes possible to realize that the same procedure is never the same procedure, even if it is technically identical. The focus on data to the exclusion of emotional variables leaves the patient only to hope that he or she "falls" into the right category. This atmosphere not only turns patients into statistics, ultimately it turns them into data.

Data can be dehumanizing. If you were described only using data points (such as height, age, or country of origin), what important characteristics would the data user miss?

_____

_____

_____

The de-differentiating effects of data are not, however, confined to the physician's office. They are part and parcel of the chronic anxiety in society. Daily, the media publish the latest results of some "scientific" discovery showing a relationship between your most feared disease and something you ingest or do, or they bring false promise of a quick fix to one of the more serious illnesses. The nerve-wracking effect on patients is many-fold:

- **The sheer amount of data is overwhelming**
- **The studies are confusing and often contradictory**
- **The data themselves are formatted in anxiety-provoking formulas that leave out emotional variables**

The propensity of such studies to induce a "failure of nerve" lies not only in their sheer volume but also in the way a regressed civilizations' focus on pathology and drive for certainty causes them to be formatted in the first place. They are always phrased in a way that stresses the damage, rather than the chances for survival.

Chronically anxious leaders tend to focus on the negative rather than on the positive, while self-differentiated leaders see the glass as half full. Think of a recent setback you experienced. What were the positives?

_____

_____

_____

_____

_____

_____

_____

_____

_____

Thought for the week:
*«The more knowledgeable one tries to become,
the more anxious one must necessarily become.»*

MONDAY ____ / ____

TUESDAY ____ / ____

WEDNESDAY ____ / ____

THURSDAY ____ / ____

FRIDAY ____ / ____

WEEKEND ____ / ____

WEEK THIRTEEN
DATA AND MANAGEMENT

Parents today can learn about techniques of parenting from programs and lectures in churches and synagogues, universities, hospitals, libraries, PTAs, and community programs at mental health institutions. Yet there is absolutely no evidence that the most successful parents are those who are most "knowledgeable" of either the "proper" techniques or the latest data on children. One would be hard-pressed to show that members of the mental health professions, who presumably have far more data than the average "lay" parent, are doing a better job of raising their children.

SELF-ASSESSMENT

I value my colleagues' degrees or certifications more than I value their experience.

○ **TRUE**   ○ **FALSE**

Parenting is no different than any other kind of "managing." The critical issues in raising children have far less to do with proper technique than with the nature of the parents' presence and the type of emotional processes they engender. When parents are willing to take responsibility for their own unworked-out relationships either with their own parents or with one another, children rarely develop serious symptoms.

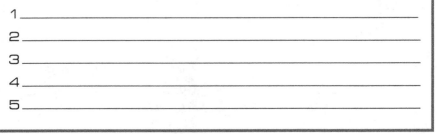

Consider other ways that parenting and managing are alike. List 5 attributes that good parents and good leaders share.

1 _____

2 _____

3 _____

4 _____

5 _____

The number of books being written today on management far exceeds the number of managers. If the data deluge puts all leaders on an anxious treadmill of pursuing more information in order to "stay on top of things," **the pursuit of information also offers family and institutional leaders an easy escape from having to deal with society's chronic anxiety as well as with their own personal being**.

Leaders are smack in the middle of an exquisite double bind: they are both overwhelmed and seduced by the data. Data becomes a substance that is at first eagerly sought and then ultimately abused. One reason that the abuse metaphor is appropriate is that all forms of addiction are related to the major themes of this book:

- Anxiety
- Lack of nerve
- Poorly differentiated self

Almost all addictions come about because of some combination of these factors.

Do you have any addictive behaviors (e.g., checking social media, streaming television, etc.)? How do these behaviors impact your ability to achieve your personal and professional goals?

_____

_____

_____

_____

_____

_____

_____

_____

The vicious cycle that is always characteristic of addiction—the fact that the reliance on the substance erodes the very strengths that have to be mobilized in order to break free from the substance—is remarkably descriptive of what has happened to America's leaders with regard to data and technique.

Those who become addicted:

- Tend to create relationships that are codependent
- Tend to see the world in a distorted reality
- Often have trouble distinguishing what is normal
- Live a life organized around their symptom
- Tend to be mired in guilt
- Are "enabled" to remain helpless by the helpfulness of co-dependent others

All of these attributes apply to the data addiction. "Kicking" any habit is difficult—**there is no quick fix for avoiding a quick fix**. Facing the pain of anxiety and growth, not denying the emotional processes that erode self-differentiation, being willing to risk and be vulnerable—these are the keys to overcoming an addiction to data, as well as the way to avoid being overwhelmed by the data deluge.

From the list above, circle the symptoms of data addiction you yourself experience, or have observed in the leaders around you. Describe the impacts of one symptom in depth: Are you guilty that you don't read as much in your field as you think you should? Does your company's leadership surround themselves with co-dependent people who will enable their behavior?

_____

_____

_____

_____

_____

Thought for the week:
«The assumption that data and techniques are
the keys to life is a major distortion of reality.»

MONDAY ____ / ____

TUESDAY ____ / ____

WEDNESDAY ____ / ____

THURSDAY ____ / ____

FRIDAY ____ / ____

WEEKEND ____ / ____

WEEK FOURTEEN
A NEW WORLDVIEW OF THE BRAIN

As debilitating and anxiety-provoking as information overload can be for anyone, and as misleading and addictive as the focus on data and technique can become for leaders especially, there is still a third aspect of our society's orientation toward data rather than emotional process that is misleading in a very fundamental way. That third aspect is our tendency to conceptualize the organ we call the brain as some kind of central processing unit.

Most researchers concur on one point: the brain takes emotional factors into account during the very process of cerebrating, not just after one has produced thoughts. **Emotions do not simply modify thinking, reasoning, or decision-making processes; they are part and parcel of the process of reasoning**. "Mental" includes feelings. The brain's method of processing data always includes emotional variables.

SELF-ASSESSMENTS

I never let feelings "cloud" my judgement.

○ **TRUE**   ○ **FALSE**

Logic and emotion are entangled processes.

○ **TRUE**   ○ **FALSE**

The tendency to equate the brain with only one of its subsystems, the cortex, leads us to assume that what we label "thinking" is primarily about the intellect. There is, in fact, a striking parallel between the way data and technique are separated out from emotional processes in our data-gathering endeavors and the way we have traditionally categorized cognitive processes and emotional processes separately.

The new awareness that the brain does not compartmentalize data and emotional process has important ramifications for the way parents and presidents are taught to conceptualize problems of leadership, such as role-modeling, emulation, and identification. Systemic understandings of the brain show how emotional processes are part of the thinking processes, leading to a more organic model of leadership itself and shifting the entire paradigm of how information is gathered, correlated, and given meaning.

Leadership, therefore, is doubly affected by these new orientations. Not only do they offer new ways of conceptualizing traditional leadership problems—from communication to motivation to resistance—but they also offer a different model for the way in which leaders and followers are connected. And they provide new criteria for what information is important, as well as for how to weigh its significance.

What role do you think emotions play in leadership?

_____

_____

_____

_____

_____

_____

_____

_____

_____

_____

_____

_____

_____

Four new maps of the brain suggest a more unified, that is, organic, orientation of this crucial organ, and show the unreality of separating out data from emotional processes in any formulations of life. Two of the maps are focused inward and have to do with the brain's "infrastructure." Two have an outward focus and have to do with the brain's relationship to the body.

They begin with a view of the brain as the repository of all evolution and therefore of the human connection to all other forms of life, itself a link to universal emotional processes. And they progress to a relational understanding that not only is the brain intimately connected with the body that houses it, but also, within any relationship system, the brain of one individual is connected to the bodies—and brains—of other individuals through its involvement in the emotional processes between them.

All the maps point to similar conclusions:

- **The brain does not contain a central processing unit for information**
- **The brain always processes emotional factors and data simultaneously**
- **Thinking always involves the self of the entire organism**

Which of the three conclusions above is most surprising to you? How does this information change the way you think (and feel) about thinking and feeling?

_____

_____

_____

_____

_____

_____

_____

Thought for the week:
«New maps of the brain constantly lead to
unification, not bifurcation.»

MONDAY ____ / ____

TUESDAY ____ / ____

WEDNESDAY ____ / ____

THURSDAY ____ / ____

FRIDAY ____ / ____

WEEKEND ____ / ____

WEEK FIFTEEN
MAP 1: THE TRIUNE BRAIN

In 1990, Dr. Paul McLean, who had studied the human brain for more than thirty years at the National Institute of Health, published *The Triune Brain*. His thesis is that the human brain has three distinct parts, each of which developed at a different stage of evolution but evolved in an interconnected fashion, with information flowing reciprocally between all three parts. The brain, in other words, is itself a history of the evolution of our species.

Other organs seem to have ceased evolving after reaching a form that fit their function. The brain, on the other hand, has kept changing its size and shape as animal life has evolved. The older brain forms that still reside beneath, or at the base of, the modern human brain are structurally and chemically identical to their forerunners.

As the base of the human brain is a bundle of nerve connections totally absent of thought processes: the "reptilian brain." Above that is the part of the brain that allows for thinking on rudimentary levels and evolved with early mammals: the "mammalian brain." It is in the mammalian brain that we find the apparatus for creating lasting relationships and therefore families. The third part of the brain is the half-inch layer at the top that most people think of as the "real" brain, the cortex and its frontal lobe, the neo-cortex. It is the cortex that is the center of intellectual activity, and the neo-cortex that allows for philosophical speculation, deep problem-solving, and intricate strategies.

SELF-ASSESSMENT

The brain is made of up three parts: reptilian, avian, and mammalian.

○ **TRUE**   ○ **FALSE**

For the most part, the cortex functions interdependently with its reptilian and mammalian precursors. This is as true in gathering data as in making decisions. The information each part processes is to some extent modified by the information simultaneously being processed by the other two parts.

WORD MATRIX

Match each part of Dr. McLean's triune brain with its function.

Reptilian brain   Nurturing and connection-making

Mammalian brain   Philosophy and judgement

Neo-cortex   Instinct

The major significance of McLean's work for leadership is its implication that while the modern human animal is capable of deep thought and can nurture and play, it also is capable of behaving in an absolutely "reptilian" manner. While that may sound simply like more evidence for the fact that human judgement is influenced by feelings, McLean's theory has a slightly different spin that creates a new perspective on reactivity, madness, and regression.

Dr. Michael Kerr compares McLean's view of the connection between the cortex and the lower parts of the brain to a driver-training car with two sets of controls. Normally, the cortex does all the steering, but when anxiety reaches certain thresholds the instinctual, reptilian systems can take over the cortex. The problem is that after the reptilian brain takes over, the cortex continues steering, assuming it's still in charge.

While matters of the intellect are products of the cortex, when conditions are right, the cortex can be working at the service of the lower brain. Madness has more to do with how people function in a relationship system than with products of their intellect. If everything is relative, in any institutional disagreement a leader cannot go around simply dismissing all disagreement as madness.

If, however, a leader focuses on the way people function in a relationship system rather than on their stated values and beliefs, he or she can develop a more objective perspective on the madness of others. The three criteria of reptilian functioning that leaders of any institution can always rely on to judge madness (of others or their own) are:

- **Interfering in the relationships of others**
- **Unceasingly trying to convert others to their own point of view**
- **Being unable to relate to people who do not agree with them**

These criteria are all products of anxiety and therefore rooted in the automatic reactivity of the reptilian brain rather than the more considered deliberations of the cortex, no matter how rationally they are phrased or how deliberately they are delivered.

Describe a time when you were driven by anxiety rather than rationality. How did this impact your decision making? How did you eventually overcome your fear?

_____

_____

_____

_____

_____

_____

_____

Thought for the week:
«When conditions are right, the cortex can be working
at the service of the lower brain.»

MONDAY _____ / _____

TUESDAY _____ / _____

WEDNESDAY _____ / _____

THURSDAY _____ / _____

FRIDAY _____ / _____

WEEKEND _____ / _____

WEEK SIXTEEN
MAPS 2 & 3

MAP 2: THE BRAIN'S INTERCONNECTIONS

Support for the interconnectedness of the brain divisions, as well as for an organic understanding of thinking, comes from another perspective also: Dr. Antonio Damasio and others who have been tracing the internal pathways of communication between various parts of the brain. Their new cartography shows that while various parts of the brain may have different functions, they do not simply act upon one another's results as much as interact all along the way, so that the data that any of these parts produces have been influenced by their interactions within the overall process. A given brain unit's contribution is not just in its structure but also in its position in the system.

Thought processes are not simply affected by emotional processes; rather, those processes are the constituent of the "intellectual" process by which information is acquired and judgements made. Biological regulation of the entire organism interlocks with reasoning and decision-making.

SELF-ASSESSMENTS

Good leaders never make emotional decisions.

○ **TRUE**   ○ **FALSE**

It is natural to weigh both logic and feeling when making a judgement.

○ **TRUE**   ○ **FALSE**

Not only are the brain's various parts interactive with one another, but the brain's connection with the body is also interactive. The brain, suggests Damasio, is "the body's captive audience." Our brains could not be grounded in reality without our bodies. Neither brain nor body interacts with the environment alone, without the participation of the other.

A major result of this research is the concept that sound judgement turns out to be related to parts of the brain that do not deal with data. In other words, being informed is not enough.

McLean and Damasio's research into the infrastructure of the brain raises many questions about the conventional understanding of intelligence that informs leadership training programs. They suggest that some kind of conceptual leap is needed beyond what has come to be termed emotional intelligence.

Damasio suggests that the brain-body connection plays a significant role in decision making. Just as leaders cannot truly separate their emotions from their data-driven thought-processes, neither can a leader separate his or herself from his/her physical surroundings. What physical factors impact your decision making? In what environment do you do your most measured thinking?

_____

_____

_____

_____

_____

_____

_____

_____

_____

MAP 3: A LIQUID NERVOUS SYSTEM

Damasio and McLean draw from an internal perspective, the relationship of brain parts to one another. There is also new brain cartography drawn from an external perspective: the relationship of the entire brain itself to other body parts if not to other bodies.

For many years the major model of our nervous systems has been electrical. A charge travels down a neuron, thereby communicating with the network next door. In recent years, however, more attention has been given to the fact that nerves also communicate with one another through liquid pathways, where neurotransmitters travel via the body's fluids and dock at receptor sites. Communication between glands and other organs throughout the body is a more systemic process than a mere matter of communication relays. **Body parts can have an impact on one another from a distance**.

This brain-body orientation understanding of the brain points to several new ways of thinking about both data-processing and leadership:

- To be effective, a "head" must find a way to be present in the body it is leading
- The nature of that presence is felt through its impact, not its messages
- If the relationship between a "head" and a body is organic rather than hierarchical, proximity and contiguity is not as important as we think
- Consultation for leaders can be viewed as biofeedback rather than a dispensing of cures

SELF-ASSESSMENT

An effective leader can affect many parts of a company simultaneously.

○ **TRUE**   ○ **FALSE**

Thought for the week:
«"Feelings are as cognitive as precepts."
– Dr. Antonio Damasio»

MONDAY _____ / _____

TUESDAY _____ / _____

WEDNESDAY _____ / _____

THURSDAY _____ / _____

FRIDAY _____ / _____

WEEKEND _____ / _____

WEEK SEVENTEEN
MAP 4: THE BRAIN AND OTHER BODIES

The notion that the brain of one body can be connected to other bodies requires a conceptual leap. That jump forward was provided by the pioneers of the family therapy movement, who began to focus on relationship processes rather than discrete personalities. People in any family or institution are connected by the emotional processes between them, and the relationship system is understood to be a self-organizing unit.

This leads logically to the conclusion that one cannot understand one body's brain without understanding the relationship of that body with other bodies. It is possible to view the thinking process of each individual in an institution as constantly interactive. Just as data are processed within the brain simultaneously along with emotional variables, so it is also possible to view the thinking in each individual part of a relationship system as being processed simultaneously in a context of reciprocal feedback.

No leader is an island. Think about the day-to-day processes that you "own." How are they impacted by those around you? How do you currently make space for feedback from those voices?

_____

_____

_____

_____

_____

_____

_____

Here are two examples of how the brain of one human being is influenced by the connection of its body to other bodies in a relationship system:

Communication: The notion that communication is essentially about ideas is basic to all training programs about leadership. Leaders in all professions are coached on how to articulate their ideas more clearly, focusing on syntax, semantics, rhetoric, and diction, rather than emotion.

A new view of the brain suggests instead that communication is itself an emotional phenomenon that depends on three inter-relational variables: direction, distance, and anxiety. The capacity of those with whom you are communicating to hear you depends on these three variables. Others can only hear you when they are moving toward you, no matter how eloquently you phrase the message. Messages in any organization come through less because of the quality of their content than because of the emotional envelope in which they are delivered.

Secrets: If most of the members of an organization are privy to a secret, the person who is not will find his or her thought processes begin to take on a paranoid tinge that has nothing to do with his or her personality.

Self-differentiated leaders must reframe their communication plans to consider the state of the listener over the intentions of the communicator. Reflect on the last time you had to communicate to a team member or group—were you more focused on their needs, or on your own desire to share something? How might the conversation have gone differently if you had put the receiver in the forefront?

_____

_____

_____

_____

The four new brain horizons described lead to a more organic definition of thinking, one that involves the functioning and the integrity of an entire being, not simply one that understands thinking as a mere mental activity. We must distinguish between "thinking" and "cerebration," which occurs in a reactive mode and should not be truly labelled thinking. The key to thinking lies in an emotional category, the differentiation of the thinker's self.

The ramification for leaders is this: the "old world" view separates data from emotional processes, while the "new world" view focuses leaders on the nature of their own presence.

SELF-ASSESSMENT

Each new view of the brain impacts the way we understand how data, emotions, and the physical world impact the way leaders think, communicate, and make decisions. So let's test what you've learned. Match the brain map to the appropriate statement.

Map 1   Thinking within a system is not individual but interactive

Map 2   The brain can be separated into 3 parts

Map 3   The brain impacts and is impacted by other organs

Map 4   The brain communicates via a liquid nervous system

It is often said that new ways of seeing must originate from outside of a system. My experience, however, is that truly novel concepts can begin from within, provided someone can get "outside" of its emotional processes. The "catch 22" is this: in order to be able to identify those emotional processes, one must be able to think differently in the first place. The capacity to "hear" new ideas in an institution depends on the capacity to avoid being automatically regulated by that system's emotional response. And the more reactive the surrounding climate, the more society in its anxious efforts will reify its models and eventually confuse them with reality itself.

Thought for the week:
«Anxiety is the static in any communication system
and can distort any message.»

MONDAY _____ / _____   **TUESDAY** _____ / _____

WEDNESDAY _____ / _____   **THURSDAY** _____ / _____

FRIDAY _____ / _____   **WEEKEND** _____ / _____

WEEK EIGHTEEN
THE FALLACY OF EMPATHY

As lofty and noble as the concept of empathy may sound, and as well-intentioned as those may be who make it the linchpin of their theories of management, society regression has too often perverted the use of empathy into a disguise for anxiety, a rationalization for the failure to define a position, and a power tool in the hands of the "sensitive."

It has generally been my experience that in any community or family discussion, those who are the first to introduce concern for empathy feel powerless and are trying to use the togetherness force of a regressed society to get those whom they perceive to have power to adapt to them. I have consistently found the introduction of the subject of "empathy" into institutional meetings to be reflective of, as well as an effort to induce, a failure of nerve among its leadership.

Does this assertion about empathy surprise you? What are your current feelings on the role of empathy in the workplace?

_____

_____

_____

_____

_____

_____

_____

_____

_____

One day I made a presentation to a large group of community leaders about my ideas on imaginative gridlock; it was illustrated with slides of maps, and was received enthusiastically by the audience. Then someone arose and said, "That was one of the most boring presentations I have ever heard, and I am deeply hurt by your ethnocentric bias."

I decided that I would respond in a way that went in the face of his sensitivities. I told him I couldn't care less about his feelings and that I was trying to present universal, challenging ideas about the orientations of stuck civilizations and the evolutionary value of adventure. "My views may not always be correct," I added, "but if anyone in the audience is having trouble getting in touch with the universal themes of human existence that I am trying to portray because of the cultural context in which I have drawn my metaphor, then there is some serious question to be raised about whose ethnocentricity is getting in the way."

Many people, even those in leadership, find facing direct confrontation challenging. How would you have responded in the situation above?

_____

_____

_____

_____

_____

_____

_____

_____

_____

_____

_____

_____

At this point another member of the audience said, "You are still avoiding his feelings." This time I responded "He may have been 'hurt,' but he wasn't damaged. My purpose here is to expand your minds with previously unimagined concepts. The previous questioner is creating a diversion by introducing political rhetoric, and I don't intend to let him steal my agenda, nor will I take responsibility for his feelings. If, on the other, he wants to express his opinions about my ideas, I will be completely open to such dialogue. **But dialogue is only possible when we can learn to distinguish feelings from opinions and recognize that the background or personality of a person is totally irrelevant to the validity of what her or she is saying.**"

I wanted to pierce the general illusions of empathy that so disorient American society today and give license to the undercutting of well-defined leadership everywhere.

SELF-ASSESSMENTS

I find myself easily sidetracked by oppositional views.

○ **TRUE**   ○ **FALSE**

My fear of confrontation impacts my ability to accomplish my goals.

○ **TRUE**   ○ **FALSE**

I sometimes feel that others take advantage of my good nature.

○ **TRUE**   ○ **FALSE**

Thought for the week:
«Societal regression has perverted
the use of empathy into a disguise for anxiety.»

MONDAY _____ / _____

TUESDAY _____ / _____

WEDNESDAY _____ / _____

THURSDAY _____ / _____

FRIDAY _____ / _____

WEEKEND _____ / _____

WEEK NINETEEN
EMPATHY VS. RESPONSIBILITY

The second emotional barrier to reorienting leadership in our time is the focus on empathy rather than responsibility. The great myth here is that feeling deeply for others increases their ability to mature and survive; its corollary is that the effort to understand another should take precedence over the endeavor to make one's own self clear. However, **the constant effort to understand or feel for another can be as invasive as any form of emotional coercion**.

While a focus on feelings would seem to be the exact opposite of a focus on data, it has an equally regressive effect on leadership. What the orientation toward data and the orientation toward feeling share in common is:

- A focus on weakness or immaturity rather than on strength
- An orientation toward others rather than toward self
- A way of avoiding issues of personal accountability

Constant calls for empathy require that leaders undertake a great deal of emotional labor, which can in turn distract from their primary objectives. Can you think of a time when a single person's emotional agenda was allowed to overtake a meeting or project discussion? What do you remember most about the meeting—the emotional outburst, or the meeting's original goal?

_____

_____

_____

_____

_____

The most deleterious effect of empathy's subversion on leaders is more fundamental. It has to do with the way we conceptualize the forces of light and darkness. **The focus on empathy rather than responsibility has contributed to a major misorientation in our society** about the nature of what is toxic to life itself, and therefore, the factors that go into survival.

On the most fundamental level, this chapter is about the struggle between good and evil, between life and death, between what is destructive and what is creative, between dependency and responsibility, and, in the deepest realms of personal existence, between what is evolutionary and what is regressive.

How do you define "responsibility"? Consider the word in both a personal and professional context.

_____

_____

_____

_____

_____

_____

_____

_____

The word *empathy* is used so often today by managers that few realize it only entered the English language in the twentieth century (compared to *sympathy*, which is 450 years old, and *compassion*, which goes back to 1340). The original intent of the word *empathy* was to convey how projecting oneself into a work of art would enable a view to appreciate better the creation being observed. It was not until after World War II that the word itself became part of common parlance, as it jumped from the realm of art appreciation to that of human relationships.

The increasing popularity of empathy over the past few decades is symptomatic of the herding/togetherness force characteristic of an anxious society. There can be no question that the notion of feeling for others, identifying with others, being responsive to others, is heartfelt humanitarian, highly spiritual, and an essential component in a leader's response repertoire.

I am concerned here not with the "true" meaning of the word *empathy* but with its use, and thus with what it has come to mean. As understood today, empathy may be a luxury afforded only to those who do not have to make tough decisions, the consequence of which will be painful to others. The focus on "need fulfillment" that so often accompanies an emphasis on empathy leaves out the possibility that what another may really "need" is not to have their needs fulfilled.

Increasing one's threshold for another's pain is often the only way the other will become motivated to increase their own threshold, thus becoming better equipped to face the challenges of life. Ultimately, organizations are able to evolve out of a state of regression not because their leaders "feel" for their followers, but because their leaders are able, by their well-defined presence, to regulate the systemic anxiety in the relationship system they are leading and to inhibit the invasiveness of those factions that would preempt its agenda. After that, they can afford to be empathic.

SELF-ASSESSMENT

Sometimes a leader's job is *not* to give people what they want.

○ **TRUE**   ○ **FALSE**

Thought for the week:
«It is not clear that feeling for others
is a more caring space than challenging them
to take responsibility for themselves.»

MONDAY _____ / _____

TUESDAY _____ / _____

WEDNESDAY _____ / _____

THURSDAY _____ / _____

FRIDAY _____ / _____

WEEKEND _____ / _____

WEEK TWENTY
HOSTILE ENVIRONMENTS

This chapter is divided into two major sections: the first is devoted to the **nature of the hostile environment** and the second to **survival in a hostile environment**. I will show that in any relationship system, all disintegrative forces have one essential characteristic in common that is totally unresponsive to empathy: their un-self-regulating invasiveness of others' spaces. Forces that are un-self-regulating can never be made to adapt toward the strength in a system by trying to understand or appreciate their nature.

In any hostile environment, whether the toxic force is outside or inside the person, **most often the critical response has less to do with the toxic factors within the system than with the response of the endangered organism**. It is responsibility, not empathy, that is the crucial variable in this equation. Most leaders require a sensitivity to the degree of chronic anxiety and the lack of self-differentiation in the system that surrounds them. The development of that ability requires that they self-regulate their own reactive mechanisms and that they muster the stamina to define themselves continually to those who lack self-regulation. Leaders must put their primary emphasis on their own continual growth and maturity.

WORD CLOUD

Circle the phrases that represent risks faced by anxiously empathic leaders.

Distracted from mission

Appearance of care

Avoidance of conflict

Followers who do not take responsibility

Focus on need fulfillment

Decreased threshold for others' pain

All entities that are destructive to other entities share one major characteristic that is totally unresponsive to empathy: *they are not capable of self-regulation.* Self-regulation may be the context for all evolutionary advances; it is part of the ongoing natural processes of creation. A lack of self-regulation holds true for viruses, malignant cells, and abusers of substances and people.

The inability of regressive entities to self-regulate is the basis for two derivative attributes that all pathogenic forces or entities have in common:

- All organisms that lack self-regulation will be *perpetually invading the space of their neighbors*
- Organisms that are unable to self-regulate *cannot learn from their experience*

When it comes to human beings, these principles are not amenable to empathy. If anything, they are strengthened by focusing on others, rather than on the self. Recognizing these principles can create a major reorientation for understanding and dealing with many of the dilemmas of leadership, particularly resistance, sabotage, perversity, and madness.

Self-differentiated leaders must be on the lookout for these behaviors both in others and in themselves. From the bullet points above, choose whichever attribute you struggle with most. When in recent memory have you exhibited this behavior? Keeping the principles of self-regulation and non-reactivity in mind, what might you have done differently?

_____

_____

_____

_____

_____

_____

VIRUSES

Critical for our discussion of the importance of self-regulation is the fact that viruses do not regulate their own behavior at any stage. Viruses have no nucleus to organize their being, and they often have no surrounding membrane that helps them differentiate their own being from other entities in their environment. In short, viruses have no *self* in any meaningful sense. They are the ultimate in reactivity, and the very essence of parasitic dependency. Their behavior and their direction are determined by what is outside rather than what is within.

Their invasiveness is not symptomatic of an attribute they possess, but it is due, rather, to what they do not possess: the ability to be self-determined in any purposeful way. They have no way to learn from previous experience. They can change, but generally speaking they do not evolve.

Viruses can be tremendously disruptive to normal life and functions, as demonstrated in recent years. Non-self-regulating people have the potential to be just as disruptive if their behaviors are not recognized by a leader. List three steps that you would take to keep a virus (or virus-like individual) from gaining traction in your workplace or community.

1 _____

_____

2 _____

_____

3 _____

_____

4 _____

_____

5 _____

_____

Thought for the week:
«As with a focus on data and technique, the focus on empathy subverts the self-differentiating process.»

MONDAY ____ / ____

....
....
....
....
....
....

TUESDAY ____ / ____

....
....
....
....
....
....

WEDNESDAY ____ / ____

....
....
....
....
....
....

THURSDAY ____ / ____

....
....
....
....
....
....

FRIDAY ____ / ____

....
....
....
....
....
....

WEEKEND ____ / ____

....
....
....
....
....
....

WEEK TWENTY-ONE
MALIGNANT CELLS

If we go up to the next level of life's organization, the cell, we find that self-regulation is critical to differentiate between life-sustaining cells and the destructive cells we call malignant. While both organisms do have a nucleus, malignant cells differ from normal cells in at least five respects, all of which are connected by the issue of self-definition and self-regulation. Normal cells:

• Differentiate from their parent cell and gain a specific identity that imbues them with purpose. Some have specific genes that cause them to gravitate toward other cells with a similar function
• Develop to a specialization stage, in which they become somatically determined, forming a colony with a particular life function that contributes to the overall functioning of the larger society
• Communicate with one another and become part of a mutually reciprocal network that regulates each one's growth, behavior, and to some extent survival
• Cease to proliferate indiscriminately during the specialization stage, propagating only offspring that have the same function as themselves. This ensures their becoming cooperative rather than competitive with the larger society
• Have a gene for self-destruction. When cells contain entities that are dangerous to the larger society, that gene can be activated

SELF-ASSESSMENT

Self-differentiated leaders should seek to embody the self-regulating characteristics of a normal cell.

○ **TRUE**　○ **FALSE**

Malignant cells differ from normal cells in all five of the following respects, and in every case the differences and their pathogenic potential are connected through issues of self-regulation and self-definition. Malignant cells:

- Either fail to develop or lose the capacity for self-definition, with the result that they remain permanently immature
- Their colonies are totally un-self-regulating
- Are rogue cells, unconnected from reciprocal networks with other cells that might influence their growth and behavior
- Reproduce uncontrollably even after they colonize. They are guilty of treason, competing with or subverting the body that gives them life
- Don't know when to quit. Seemingly capable of purposeless immortality, the only way malignant cells self-destruct is by taking their host with them
- Malignant cells operate without any responsiveness to a larger association. At no time, however, can their selfishness be attributed to intent; as with viruses, their selfishness has to do with a lack of self.

Teenagers are often held up as the epitome of selfish society members. Their behavior is unregulated as they work to discover their own sense of self, as human beings are not lucky enough to have their purpose pre-programmed, like a cell! Imagine what your company would be like if it were staffed by teenagers. Would there be a big change? Or are similarly disruptive forces already at work?

_____

_____

_____

_____

_____

The combination of these five interconnected characteristics of malignant cells creates the regressive process we have come to call cancer. These same five factors among human organisms in any institution create the emotional processes that are also malignant.

In neither case can health be restored by a quick fix or through understanding. The understanding that is needed is how to prevent the progression of their invasiveness. The ultimate similarity between organisms and organizations is that, unlike diseases "caused" by the continued presence of some chronically troublemaking noxious agent, as in the case of a virus or bacterium, malignant processes continue to subvert even though the toxic agent that initiated the original misdirection is no longer around to continue energizing the pathology.

In this metaphor, leaders are called to act as doctors for their ailing organizations. Their true duty is not to ameliorate the symptoms of an illness (empathy) but to identify the source and halt the illness's ongoing spread (responsibility). As you consider your role as a leader, what are the symptoms, and what are the sources, in the organization around you?

_____

_____

_____

_____

_____

_____

_____

_____

_____

Thought for the week:
«Malignancies at any level of life's organization occur when an essential life process has been perverted.»

MONDAY _____ / _____

TUESDAY _____ / _____

WEDNESDAY _____ / _____

THURSDAY _____ / _____

FRIDAY _____ / _____

WEEKEND _____ / _____

WEEK TWENTY-TWO
ORGANISMS

Now let us go up a step to the level of human organisms. Members of institutions who never quit being difficult—do they not behave like viruses or malignant cells? Do they not function as though they had no nucleus, as though they were more reactive than inner-directed? Are they not more parasitic than symbiotic? Does not their invasiveness contaminate the family or institution of which they are a part? Will being sensitive to their needs regulate their invasiveness or instill greater self-definition?

No organization is completely free of un-self-regulating individuals, but the disruptive presence of these reactive persons can be mitigated through courageous leadership. Practice these mantras to defend against the influences of energy-sapping, chronically anxious colleagues.

I will not allow others to divert my course.

I will not allow others to take without giving back in the name of "empathy."

I will not define myself in opposition to others.

One can only be consistent with chronically troubling individuals when one is focused on oneself, not on the random perturbations of the un-self-regulating other. The former is what leadership is about; the latter allows followers to set the agendas. Leaders must be able to concentrate on the preservation of their own integrity rather than on the effort to "mutate" the other. This shift in focus from the other to their own self also affects their stamina. Once leaders are oriented towards their own welfare rather than trying to be empathic to the troublesome other, their stamina begins to increase.

This comparison to viruses and malignant cells extends to all forms of organized life. Listed below are ten interrelated characteristics of potentially "malignant" members of institutions that are particularly troublesome to leaders.

1. They tend to be easily hurt by "injustice-collectors," slow healers who are given to victim attitudes.
2. They tend to idolize their leaders until their unrealistic expectations fail, whereupon they are quick to "crucify" their gods.
3. Their intent is often "innocently provocative"; they do not see themselves as bent on destruction.
4. Their repertoire of responses is limited to being "on" or "off," linear, black-and-white.
5. They focus on procedure and rituals, and they get stuck on the content of issues rather than being able to view the surrounding emotional processes that are spawning the issues.
6. Light and truth is toxic to their nature; they thrive in the darkness of conspiracy.
7. They are driven by their reptilian brains: they have a high degree of reactivity, a narrow range of responses, and they are always serious.
8. They tend to interfere in the relationships of others.
9. They are easily panicked into group-think.
10. They are relentless and totally invulnerable to insight.

This is not to say that for such individuals there is no hope for rehabilitation. But empathy alone will never promote the self-organization necessary for learning from experience; that can only come about when they are told that if they want to be a part of the community, they must adapt to it, not the other way around.

Recognizing the impacts of chronically anxious colleagues can be crucial, but becoming a self-differentiated leader ultimately requires turning one's focus inward to your own vision and goals. Take a moment to revisit your goals from week one. Have any changed? How are you progressing?

_____

_____

_____

_____

_____

_____

_____

_____

_____

_____

Nurturing growth in un-regulated or troublesome individuals always follows two principles:

- **Stay out if its way**
- **Do not let it "overgrow" you**

You cannot "grow" another by will or technique. Secondly, there must be self-differentiation in the leader before there can be self-differentiation in the follower. I have continually found that when parents can make the transition in their orientation from focusing on how to grow their children to how to prevent their children from overgrowing them, their children do begin to grow—that is, grow up—and so do the parents.

Thought for the week:
«One can only be consistent when
one is focused on oneself.»

MONDAY _____ / _____

TUESDAY _____ / _____

WEDNESDAY _____ / _____

THURSDAY _____ / _____

FRIDAY _____ / _____

WEEKEND _____ / _____

WEEK TWENTY-THREE
INSTITUTIONS

On this level of life's organization, the entities that are most pathogenic lack self-regulation and self-definition. Both their poorly defined boundaries and their lack of integrity give them a parasitic quality that is ultimately immoral. Both organized crime and subversive organizations are like viruses in the sense that they do not develop out of their own structures but are dependent on others, and their direction comes not from some nucleus that supplies them with self-organization but is a reaction to the environment that surrounds them.

It goes without saying that such institutions are almost never able, or willing, to integrate their experiences in a way that enables them to develop a more enriched individuality. They might get larger, but they do not "grow" or evolve. They certainly do not know when to quit, much less die.

SELF-ASSESSMENTS

It's important to understand the health of the organizations that you are involved in. Did you answer no to any of the following? If so, you organization may be troubled by some regressive factors.

My organization has a strong, self-determined vision and mission.

○ **TRUE**　○ **FALSE**

My organization benefits society at large.

○ **TRUE**　○ **FALSE**

My organization has positive reciprocal relationships with other bodies or organizations.

○ **TRUE**　○ **FALSE**

My organization's mission and structure have evolved over time.

○ **TRUE**　○ **FALSE**

The form of human colonization that functions most similarly to a virus or a malignant cell is the totalitarian nation. No human entity is more invasive to the lives of its citizens and the space of its neighbors. They infect what they touch, and they seek to replicate their own being. They certainly do not know when to quit.

It is this same lack of self-regulation and the inner integrity required for self-definition that makes totalitarian nations notoriously untrustworthy of agreements and treaties. Yet they may be no more immoral than a virus, for their perpetual immorality may stem less from an evil intention than the fact that they are incapable, constitutionally, of the self-regulation required.

This brings us back to the irrelevance of empathy in the face of a relentless force. History is full of democratic countries trying unsuccessfully to stave off conflict with invasive nations by trying to appease them. The reluctance of democracies to go to war against totalitarian nations is identical to the reluctance of members of any institution to stand up to the "troublemaker." The invasive forces get their way because the "peace-loving" lack the will to confront them.

Leadership strategies and foreign policy have many similarities. How do yours overlap?

_____

_____

_____

_____

_____

_____

_____

_____

_____

_____

Pathogens do not have the power to create pathology on their own. There must also be a lack of regulation in the host. In other words, it is not merely the presence of the pathogen that causes pathology, but also the response of the organism that "hosts" it.

Imagine that the cells of an organ receive an early warning signal that a rogue cancer cell is coming down the pike. Knowing that metastasis can only occur if the healthy cells allow the malignant cells to puncture their own membranes, they huddle together and agree; no one is to allow this thing in. But after a while some of the cells realize the metastasis has begun. They look at the other cells, now dying, and say, "What's the matter with you? Why did you let it invade our space?"

And the cells that let the cancer cell in say helplessly, "We were watching it swim alone out there. It just seemed so lonely—we started to feel sorry for it."

While the examples above may seem extreme, much is at risk if an organization allows the immature and un-self-regulated to take the helm. Think of all the lives and industries your organization touches. Who would be impacted if the leadership of your organization were led astray?

_____

_____

_____

_____

_____

_____

_____

_____

_____

Thought for the week:
«For pathogens, self-regulation is not a matter of choice; they can't help it. But the host can.»

MONDAY ____ / ____

TUESDAY ____ / ____

WEDNESDAY ____ / ____

THURSDAY ____ / ____

FRIDAY ____ / ____

WEEKEND ____ / ____

WEEK TWENTY-FOUR
SURVIVAL IN A HOSTILE ENVIRONMENT

Whether we are considering the self-defense of a nation or the cohesiveness of an organization, the key to survival is the ability of the "host" to recognize and limit the invasiveness of its viral or malignant components. If lack of self-regulation is the essential characteristic of organisms that are destructive, it is the presence of self-regulatory capacity that is critical to the health, survival, and evolution of an organization.

That is precisely the function of a leader within any institution: to provide that regulation through his or her non-anxious, self-defined presence. Pathology is always a relational phenomenon, and the determining variable is usually the integrity of the host. It both depends upon, and contributes to, the self-defining nature of an organism. This principle, too, is totally independent of empathic initiatives.

A leader is responsible for protecting his or her own ability to lead. How confident are you in your ability to resist the forces of hostile environment? How will you shore yourself up against the distractions of empathy?

_____

_____

_____

_____

_____

_____

_____

_____

_____

The previous section was about the irrelevance of empathy to appreciating what is toxic to life; this section will demonstrate that the capacity for, or the demonstration of, empathy is also irrelevant to, or often distracting from, the resources that go into survival. Those resources are applicable to all human organisms irrespective of gender, race, class, and age.

Rate where you stand in your current repertoire of defenses against hostile environments.

- A healthy dose of self (/5)
- The capacity to take responsibility for one's condition (/5)
- Resiliency (/5)
- Self-regulation of anxious reactivity (/5)

Where do you need work? Set a plan to shore up your defenses. List your first steps.

_____

_____

_____

_____

_____

_____

_____

_____

_____

_____

_____

_____

_____

Toward the end of World War II, the USS Indianapolis was torpedoed suddenly by a Japanese submarine in the middle of the Japan Sea. The ship went down before a mayday message could be sent, and 800 men were left helpless in the hostile environment of a salty sea, man-eating sharks, and a scorching sun.

Although they knew it was to their advantage to stay close to one another, some of the men swam away from the group and, either willingly or out of madness, gave themselves up to the sharks. It was the greatest loss of life on one ship since Pearl Harbor. "How do you explain that?" I asked.

The lack of presence evinced by the captain that led to his ship's being torpedoed might have contributed to a lack of social cohesion among the men in the water and thereby robbed them of an integrating force that might have optimized their potential for survival. He was later court-martialed.

Put yourself in the place of the Indianapolis' captain. What would you have said or done to unite your men and minimize loss of life?

_____

_____

_____

_____

_____

_____

_____

_____

_____

_____

_____

Thought for the week:
«Empathy alone will never promote the self-organization necessary for learning from experience.»

MONDAY _____ / _____

TUESDAY _____ / _____

WEDNESDAY _____ / _____

THURSDAY _____ / _____

FRIDAY _____ / _____

WEEKEND _____ / _____

WEEK TWENTY-FIVE

IMAGINATIVE CAPACITY AND THE ODDS FOR SURVIVAL

It may be said unequivocally that whenever anyone is in extremis, their chances of survival are far greater when their horizons are formed of projected images from their own imagination, rather than being limited by what they can actually see. Or, to reverse it, to the extent the horizons of individuals in extremis are limited to what they can actually see, their chances of survival are far less than if their horizons include projected images from their own imagination. Even the thinking processes that lead one to assume that one's life situation is in extremis are partially determined by the breadth of one's horizons at the time—which correlates with one's imaginative capacity and sense of adventure.

This principle of survival is supported by the experiences of many who survived the Nazi Holocaust and is perhaps also indicative of many who were far-seeing enough to get out. **Both those who have written about their survival and those who have researched the survivors note a capacity to see beyond the barbed wire.** Such vision obviously does not guarantee survival, but it does seem to have maximized the chances for it.

SELF-ASSESSMENTS

I have a resilient mindset, even in the face of adversity.

○ **TRUE**   ○ **FALSE**

It is natural for me to reframe a problem when no positive outcomes are immediately forthcoming.

○ **TRUE**   ○ **FALSE**

There are always three factors involved in survival, no matter how toxic the environment. One is the **physical reality**, the second is **dumb luck**, and the third is **the response of the organism**, which can often modify the influence of the first two. The relationship of these three factors can be imagines as dials on an amplifier, with survival depending on the overall mix. In most crises, the first two dials are rarely going full blast—but when an individual's anxiety is high, he or she will tend to ignore the third dial and focus only on the first two.

When life crises are viewed in terms of systems thinking rather than linear thinking, outcomes other than mere capitulation or escape become possible. One such outcome is the mobilization of an organism's resources, such as resiliency, determination, self-regulation, and stamina. A second is transformation of the organism, which includes a higher capacity to deal with future crises. And a third is modification of the toxicity of the environment. **Our response is always far more influential than our chronically anxious society leads us to believe, and it is sometimes the ultimately determinative variable.**

Do you ever leave things to chance? When things don't go your way, do you believe it "just wasn't meant to be"? Consider your variables—are there any additional factors you can control to influence the outcome in your favor? If not, think creatively for different paths with the potential to yield the results you seek.

_____

_____

_____

_____

_____

_____

_____

An enormous number of problems that leaders have to deal with are crises produced by their own differentiation. To the extent one focuses solely on how painful a situation is, there is no way to judge whether things are getting worse or really improving. Despite the fact that things seem to be getting worse, that is, more toxic, the entire system may also be adapting for the better. Recognizing that can help keep anxiety down..

If a leader who has sought help can be taught how to stay in touch with the reactive group without taking their issues so seriously that he or she is thrown off course, increased differentiation can become a form of leadership that often will result in the rest getting over what ails them. This can turn the pattern of adaptation toward the one who is becoming better differentiated, thus affecting the evolution of the entire "colony."

One bad apple may spoil the bunch, but one well-differentiated leader can also lift an entire organization up over time. Write three ways you plan to commit to assist your institution through differentiation in the next six months.

I commit to

_____

_____

_____

I commit to

_____

_____

_____

I commit to

_____

_____

_____

Thought for the week:
«Many battles can be won simply by not giving up.»

MONDAY _____ / _____

....
....
....
....
....

TUESDAY _____ / _____

....
....
....
....
....

WEDNESDAY _____ / _____

....
....
....
....
....

THURSDAY _____ / _____

....
....
....
....
....

FRIDAY _____ / _____

....
....
....
....

WEEKEND _____ / _____

....
....
....
....

WEEK TWENTY-SIX
THE FALLACIES OF SELF

Half a billion years ago, life "exploded" on this planet, but an even "bigger" evolutionary explosion took place on planet Earth a billion years prior to the formation of species, with enormous consequences for the eventual development of leadership and self.

The "Big Bang" of evolution was the arrival of the *eukaryotes*, the first cells to contain a nucleus. The possession of a nucleus enabled this "new kid on the block" to increase greatly its genetic content, eventually giving life a far richer complexity of choices. Prior to that evolutionary leap, reproduction was not in service of diversity. For two billion years prior, these cells' predecessors, *prokaryotes*, lacked a nucleus and tended to clone life on this planet. The meaning of self was narrow, and leadership was an irrelevant proposition.

The arrival of the eukaryotes marked the beginning of individuality, as well as the struggle to preserve it. Imagine, therefore, the effect that the appearance of the first eukaryotes had on the balance between self and togetherness in the world of the prokaryotes.

SELF-ASSESSMENTS

The concept of "self" evolved simultaneously with the concept of life.

○ **TRUE**   ○ **FALSE**

Progress is disruptive to the status quo.

○ **TRUE**   ○ **FALSE**

To this day, wherever protoplasm colonizes, the basic tension between the lifestyles of the "prokaryotes" and the "eukaryotes" continues. The struggle between the forces for playing it safe and the forces for the preservation of individuality, between a creativity that adds new dimensions to life or a reproduction that simply reproduces, is omnipresent. Regression, therefore, usually sides with the "prokaryotes": with those who

- Compromise individuality by their narrow repertoire of responses
- Have a limited capacity for complexity and creativity
- Take an approach to togetherness aimed at fusion, not differentiation
- Focus on safety and survival rather than growth and change

When the first eukaryotes arrived, evolution leaped forward because life decided to no longer play it safe. The new creative process engendered by dividing nuclei also created far more potential for "mistakes" (mutations) than the more predictable "like father, like son" approach, but evidently life decided that mistakes were a small price to pay for the rewards that novelty could bring.

Fear of failure prevents many from pursuing risky but potentially fruitful endeavors. In the space below, outline your typical risk-reward assessment. What factors need to be in place for a risk to be potentially "worth it" to you?

_____

_____

_____

_____

_____

_____

We will explore the third emotional barrier that has to be crossed before leadership in America can be free to venture in "harm's way." **That barrier is the association of self with autocracy and narcissism rather than with integrity and individuality.** This negative orientation toward self is a natural spin-off of a chronically anxious society's focus on pathology rather than strength. This distorted focus contaminates all thinking about individuality and eventually extends to a counter-evolutionary perspective on leadership. That is because those who lack self-definition will always perceive those who are well-defined to be "headstrong."

WORD CLOUD

Match each true leadership quality on the left with its anxious partner on the right.

Brave	Single-minded
Aggressive	Egotistical
Imaginative	Hostile
Principled	Dreamer
Self-assured	Foolhardy

The illusion underlying this third emotional barrier to well-differentiated leadership is the facile "peace over progress" assumption that communities will get along when everyone stops being "selfish."

Thought for the week:
«"If I am me because you are you, and you are me
because I am me, then I am nothing, and you are
nothing." –Yiddish proverb»

MONDAY _____ / _____

TUESDAY _____ / _____

WEDNESDAY _____ / _____

THURSDAY _____ / _____

FRIDAY _____ / _____

WEEKEND _____ / _____

WEEK TWENTY-SEVEN
MORE FALLACIES OF SELF

Well-meaning efforts to eliminate the evils of selfishness by eliminating self can have as regressive an effect on a community as taking away self by force. Far from being antagonistic to the purposes of community, **the expression of self in a leader is what makes the evolution of community possible**. This principle applies equally well to partnerships, institutions, corporations, or nations, irrespective of gender, race, culture, or era.

Well-defined self in a leader—what I call self-differentiation—is not only critical to effective leadership, it is precisely the leadership characteristic that is most likely to promote the kind of community that preserves the self of its members. Lack of morality has to do with invasiveness, not strength; with lack of integrity, not power.

Ask yourself: Am I afraid to be perceived as powerful? What are the challenges that come with being seen as strong? What are some potential rewards?

_____

_____

_____

_____

_____

_____

_____

_____

_____

The twin problems confronting leadership in our society today, the failure of nerve and the desire for a quick fix, are not the result of overly strong self but of weak or no self. While there certainly is reason to guard against capricious, autocratic leadership in any form, democratic institutions have far more to fear from lack of self in their leaders than from too much strength in the executive power.

Indeed, that is precisely one of the major advantages of democratically based institutions: they can reap the benefits of imaginative, aggressive, energetic leadership far less perilously than totalitarian societies. This was the view of Alexander Hamilton and James Madison when they wrote the *Federalist Papers*, to support the "colonization" of the thirteen colonies. The American form of democracy, as structured by the Constitution of 1789, is that form of government that most corresponds to the way life itself worked out these essential tensions of existence.

The togetherness advantages of a larger organism were brought about in a way that preserved the integrity of the states. Therefore, when leaders anywhere in America work to preserve individuality, their own or others', they stand on two traditions: the processes that gave rise to our nation and the processes that gave rise to our species.

SELF-ASSESSMENT

Preservation of the self supports preservation of the community out of which the self developed.

○ **TRUE**   ○ **FALSE**

I have divided the fallacies of self into two sections. The first charts a new orientation of self by removing it from the abstractions of philosophy and psychology and rooting it instead in the natural history of life. As life has moved from simpler to more complex forms, it has continually been confronted by a tension between individuality and togetherness, but as organisms become more complex, life has always resolved that tension with regard to the integrity of the cell lineages and with regard to the organism itself.

In the second sections I will present a view of self, consistent with these biological and political perspectives, that is applicable to all personal relationships as well as essential to well-differentiated leadership. I will show how CEOs and presidents can be self-"ish" without be selfish.

On the broadest scale, the preservation of self in its leaders is a society's greatest protection against descending into counter-evolutionary mode. It is only the emergence of self in its leadership that can enable any institution or nation to evolve out of a regression.

Time to check in – you're just over halfway through! Review the critical issues of leadership that can mark the difference between a chronically anxious "leader" and a well-differentiated one.

- The capacity to "go it alone"
- The ability to recognize and extricate oneself from emotional binds
- The folly of trying to will others to change
- The modifying potential of the non-anxious presence
- The ramifying power of endurance in crisis
- The self-regulation necessary for dealing with reactive sabotage
- The factors in the leader's own being that make for his or her own stress

Thought for the week:
«The integrity of a community is assured only when it can preserve the integrity of its leader.»

MONDAY _____ / _____

....
....
....
....
....

TUESDAY _____ / _____

....
....
....
....
....

WEDNESDAY _____ / _____

....
....
....
....
....

THURSDAY _____ / _____

....
....
....
....
....

FRIDAY _____ / _____

....
....
....
....
....

WEEKEND _____ / _____

....
....
....
....
....

WEEK TWENTY-EIGHT
A NATURAL HISTORY OF THE SELF

The notion of "self" has been pondered for centuries by philosophers, psychologists, theologians, and political theorists. This notion, however, has tended to think about self as a concept that occupies our minds rather than as an entity that occupies space. When we talk about a person's ability to achieve "self-realization" it is understood in terms of their inner being or yearnings.

While this way of thinking about self is useful, it tends to lose touch with individuality as more than a philosophical concept, but a category of existence that has substantive reality and that has been an essential force in the natural processes of life since its beginnings. The effort to be one's self lines one up with what has enabled life to develop and survive since creation.

Define your "self," in the conventional sense of the word. Who are you on the inside? What are thoughts and yearnings? We'll come back to this in a bit.

_____

_____

_____

_____

_____

_____

_____

_____

_____

_____

Since its beginnings, life has gone through at least eight major transitions of complexity, during which a new form became the basic unit that the selective forces in the environment acted upon. At every transition, however, life learned to benefit from the new, more complex unit without sacrificing the integrity of the previous unit that enabled the new form to come into being. If we trace the progression of complexity across these eight major transitions we find that the preservation of individuality (self) was as critical to the evolution of life as the forming of new communities. These eight major transitions are:

- Chemicals found a way of reproducing their own form, so we have the initial appearance of self-replicating molecules
- Out of that set of self-replicating molecules, those that consisted of the base acids of DNA began to connect up into genes
- Some of the genes began to link to produce chromosomes
- Chromosomes began to become enclosed within membranes, forming the first prokaryote cells
- Eukaryote cells, with their nuclei, arrived
- Eukaryote cells aggregated to form the first living communities, multicellular organisms
- Various cells began to differentiate, with a division of labor, then further aggregated into tissues and organs
- Multicellular organisms diversified into species, beginning the line of descent that eventually led to mammals, then hominids, then families, and ultimately the forms of colonized protoplasm we call societies, cultures, communities, institutions, and nations

As these life forms became larger and more complex, a mutuality of self-interest arose in which both the smaller unit and the more complex system into which it had been incorporated worked for the survival of one another. To the extent that the smaller unit helped the larger unit, the larger unit, by surviving, ensured the survival of the smaller unit. **It was to the advantage of the smaller unit to work to preserve the larger unit's integrity, because those smaller units were more likely to survive.**

How does the description above mirror the experience of an individual within a corporation? If a leader is unable to unite individuals toward a single vision, how does this impact the health of the organization and its people?

_____

_____

_____

_____

_____

_____

_____

_____

_____

_____

_____

Incorporated units were willing to give up some control of their fate (sovereignty) in order to take advantage of a togetherness that optimized their struggle with the environment. However, since the larger unit's capacity for survival benefited from the richness it obtained by incorporating the smaller units, life did not violate the integrity of the previous form.

Thought for the week:
«Life has evolved in terms of the ways
the past is always present in the present.»

MONDAY _____ / _____

TUESDAY _____ / _____

WEDNESDAY _____ / _____

THURSDAY _____ / _____

FRIDAY _____ / _____

WEEKEND _____ / _____

WEEK TWENTY-NINE
DIFFERENTIATION

With the arrival of the eukaryote (nucleus-bearing) cell, the struggle for the preservation of individuality intensified, both internally and externally. It was necessary to keep cell lineages within them from competing with the larger organism that had incorporated them, and it was also necessary for individual cells, as well as multicellular units, to defend themselves from being taken over by other competing cells and organisms. **The perseveration of individuality, therefore, also required the development of a system of recognition, a means of knowing the self from the non-self.**

Somatic determinism, wherein only specific genes turn on within a cell in order to maintain the nature of the cell's relationship to other cells within a larger organism, solved the first problem. Once that has occurred, a cell is said to have *differentiated*. It now has individuality. But to prevent its individuality from leading to chaos or anarchy, once that cell has differentiated to a specific function it can no longer produce offspring that have the capacity to produce a competing organism.

The functioning of individuals in any institution is not determined by their nature (personality) but by their position within a relationship system, as well as by what other "cells" will permit them to do.

SELF-ASSESSMENTS

The integrity of an individual must never be interfered with, even if it negatively impacts the health of the larger organism.

○ **TRUE**   ○ **FALSE**

An organism requires a balance of cooperation and independence to function optimally.

○ **TRUE**   ○ **FALSE**

The second problem for the preservation of individuality—being invaded or parasitized by another organism—was solved with the development of the capacity of cells and organisms to mount a defense against what is "not-self." But a system of recognition had to come first. This capacity to "avoid foreign entanglements" evolved into the immune response and perhaps also into consciousness. This capacity aided in the formation of species, families, and communities.

What is the "business" equivalent of an immune response? How does your organization currently respond to threats to its mission or essential functions? What part do or can you play in those efforts?

_____

_____

_____

_____

_____

_____

_____

_____

_____

_____

_____

_____

_____

_____

_____

_____

_____

For life to evolve, all newly developed forms of togetherness must ultimately be in the service of a more enriched individuality, and not the other way around. This, after all, is the essential difference between democracy and autocracy.

Each of the following five principles guided the framers of the U.S. Constitution as they endeavored to accomplish what is enshrined in the motto on the back of our coinage—*E Pluribus Unum*, "Out of many, one." These principles are:

- Mutuality of self-interest between smaller and larger units
- A surrender of fate (sovereignty) among the smaller units in a bargain that guarantees advantages
- The formation of a new, more complex union
- Multigenerational influence
- Limitations that create checks and balances on the power of the various entities

Consider the checks and balances in place in your organization. Does one party—either the individual or the larger corporate entity—have more power than the other? If yes, what is the impact of this imbalance?

_____

_____

_____

_____

_____

_____

_____

_____

_____

_____

_____

Thought for the week:
«Out of many, one.»

MONDAY _____ / _____

TUESDAY _____ / _____

WEDNESDAY _____ / _____

THURSDAY _____ / _____

FRIDAY _____ / _____

WEEKEND _____ / _____

WEEK THIRTY
THE POLITICS OF SELF

The struggle between individuality and togetherness is part and parcel of the structuring of organizations. And **it is a critical component of leadership if leaders are to be leaders**. Yet individuality is suspect when it comes to human institutions. It is not necessary to have dictators to destroy the integrity of a democratic society. One only has to keep escalating the togetherness—promoting anxiety so that individuality is not only squelched but instinctively feared.

The evolution of society requires that the force of individuality and togetherness be kept in balance. But when that balance goes beyond certain thresholds, as occurs in periods of chronic anxiety, we wind up with devolutionary extremes: totalitarianism or anarchy; tyranny or tumors. How, therefore, are leaders to get past this third emotional barrier, the pathologizing of the self?

SELF-ASSESSMENTS

Rate three areas of your life on balance of Friedman's extremes. *Which system in your life most needs a well-differentiated leader to restore balance?*

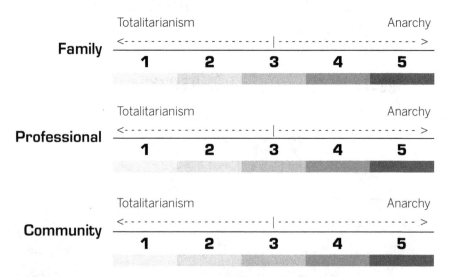

Family

Totalitarianism — Anarchy

1 2 3 4 5

Professional

Totalitarianism — Anarchy

1 2 3 4 5

Community

Totalitarianism — Anarchy

1 2 3 4 5

Success here is basic to the capacity to cross the other barriers of data and empathy. It is only when self is valued that leaders can be less at the mercy of the data/technique deluge, no less its addictive properties. **It is only when leaders value self that they can recognize the importance of making their own self-definition more crucial than feeling for others.**

When leaders value true self, they can keep it from being eroded by the chronic anxiety of a society in regression. They can muster the self-regulation necessary for countering the sabotage that will greet them, ironically, in direct relation to the extent that they value and express their self. It is this latter conundrum that so often takes leaders by surprise, just when they are functioning best.

How are parents and presidents to treasure and preserve self without worrying that they are being narcissistic or autocratic?

Think of a leader who inspires you. What methods does this leader employ to motivate others to act on their behalf? Are you using these methods in your own interactions with others?

_____

_____

_____

_____

_____

_____

_____

_____

_____

_____

_____

_____

Given the crucial value of self to the evolution of our species, how shall we explain that the word *selfish* is one of the only words in the English language where an addition of the suffix "-ish" turns an otherwise neutral noun into a pejorative label? Blueish, pinkish, and bookish are all neutral.

The grammatical uniqueness of *selfish* reflects the ambivalence inherent in the reality of self. Whether we are considering families, institutions, or whole nations, self is both desired and feared, praised and denigrated, stolen and surrendered. By its mere connectedness to another word, "self" can modify the other word's meaning positively or negatively.

WORD CLOUD

Positive

Self-assertive
Self-possessed
Self-assured
Self-made
Self-starter

Negative

Self-denial
Self-sacrifice
Self-effacement
Self-renunciation
Selfless

Look back at your description of self in Week Twenty-Eight. Can you add any of the above "self"-descriptors to your overview? Circle the selves (both positive and negative) that apply.

_____

_____

_____

_____

_____

_____

Thought for the week:
«Someone always has to go first!»

MONDAY _____ / _____   **TUESDAY** _____ / _____

....

....

....

....

....

WEDNESDAY _____ / _____   **THURSDAY** _____ / _____

....

....

....

....

....

FRIDAY _____ / _____   **WEEKEND** _____ / _____

....

....

....

....

....

WEEK THIRTY-ONE
THE IMPACT OF TOGETHERNESS ON SELF

The emphasis on togetherness is not something that can be willed. It isn't even necessary to will it. It will work for leaders to the extent that the system remains well-differentiated. The stress for leaders lies in their efforts to will togetherness—which is equally true in marriage, partnerships, and business institutions. People need one another, and that can be made to work for leaders.

Within the togetherness force, it is important to distinguish between the apparent individuality that is really reactivity to the other (and thus a manifestation of fused togetherness) and the genuine acceptance of difference. Whether we are talking about eukaryotes or marriage relationships, the pressures and the tendencies to lose one's sense of self are great, and all the more so in a regressed society. The forces for individuality must be more vigilant.

Friedman posits that the forces of togetherness feel "more natural" than the forces of individuality. Do you agree? In your own leadership journey, does it feel more natural to assert your own ideas and visions, or is it easier to go along with the desires of others?

_____

_____

_____

_____

_____

_____

_____

Herein lies a complication, a conundrum: anyone who wishes to advance our species or an institution must possess qualities that those who have little sense of self will perceive as narcissistic. "Arrogant," "headstrong," and "cold" will be the terms used against any person who tries to be more himself or herself.

SELF-ASSESSMENTS

If others believe I am selfish, I must be doing something wrong.

○ **TRUE**   ○ **FALSE**

Someone always has to go first!

○ **TRUE**   ○ **FALSE**

Good leaders are universally well-liked.

○ **TRUE**   ○ **FALSE**

Society regression reinforces the dysfunction of a system's togetherness or immaturity. To be a good leader, one must both have and embody a vision of where one wants to go. It is not a matter of knowing or believing one is right; it is a matter of taking the first step.

There is a way of understanding the self that leads to integrity and well-differentiated community rather than narcissism, isolation, and lack of feeling. It is be found in the latest understanding of the immune system, which turns out to be far less connected to self-defense than to integrity.

Up until the mid-1960s, immunity had been thought of primarily in terms of a system of defenses that the body mobilized against foreign invaders. More recently, however, the immune system has come to be seen primarily as the source of an organism's integrity, developed out of the organism's need to distinguish self from non-self.

This increased understanding changed other notions as well, so that the destruction of what is not self is seen to be a by-product of the capacity to recognize what is toxic. The very possibility of the existential category of self may have been made possible by the rise of an immune response, which is the capacity to recognize and distinguish what is foreign.

"Toxic" personalities play a role in the dysfunction of any group, whether familiarly, socially, or professionally. What characteristics mark someone's behavior out as toxic? What is the best way that you have found to minimize the impact of their behavior on the larger group?

_____

_____

_____

_____

_____

_____

_____

_____

Thought for the week:
«The well-differentiated leader will always have to be
the one to take the initiative to enhance
the functioning of the togetherness.»

MONDAY _____ / _____   **TUESDAY** _____ / _____

WEDNESDAY _____ / _____   **THURSDAY** _____ / _____

FRIDAY _____ / _____   **WEEKEND** _____ / _____

WEEK THIRTY-TWO
THE POWER OF THE IMMUNE RESPONSE

There are four characteristics of the immune system that have parallels for human relationships. These four characteristics, each of which can be understood in terms of self and human relationships, are:

- It makes possible the category of self.
- It does not come full-blown at birth, but grows from response to challenge.
- It is necessary for closeness, proximity, and love.
- It can be perverted to attack the host.

Reflect on a challenging experience in your past. How did it help to define your sense of self?

_____

_____

_____

_____

_____

_____

When organisms of a species that lacks an immune system touch, they fuse as one. That is why the immune system is considered to have a more fundamental role than protection: namely, it provides an organism with integrity. But if its main activity appears to be protection, the immune system is also essential to love, since without "immunity" not only would we never dare touch, but many of us would lose self if we got too close because of emotional fusion.

And many of do "lose it," that is lose self when we get too close. Indeed, it may be stated that **the major relational problem for our species is not getting together; the problem is preserving self in a close relationship**. No human on planet Earth does that well.

I know how to teach any organizational member how to make another member of that system dysfunctional. I would simply teach them how to overfunction in the other's space. **When one overfunctions in another's space, it can cause another's being to disintegrate.** That emotional phenomenon occurs daily across our planet.

Have you ever worked for or with a micromanager? How did their "closeness" to your work impact your confidence in and ownership over the task at hand?

_____

_____

_____

_____

_____

_____

_____

_____

_____

_____

_____

Another lesson to be learned from immunology concerns inner consistency. The immune system does not reside in one organ, nor is it positioned in some advantageous location. The importance of this evolutionary development is connection. Neurotransmitters are chemicals that communicate though the neural network, communicating information and emotions throughout the self.

A human organism's immune system is not given at birth. People are initially without an immune response other than the antibodies they receive through their mother's placenta. The immune system develops in response to challenge. Antibodies have the capacity to discriminate what is non-self and potentially threatening to an organism from that which is self. Once set in place, this immune system generally performs.

But sometimes things go wrong. Under certain conditions the immune system fails to distinguish friend from foe and attacks the self of the body instead. More and more diseases have been implicated in this hawkish behavior. It has been suggested, however, that this autoimmune response only occurs in the presence of a threat.

The immune response is the capacity to distinguish self from non-self. While that may not seem hard to do intellectually, it is not always easy to do emotionally. **Knowing where one begins and another ends is a fundamental human problem.**

Has someone ever mistaken you for an adversary when you were only trying to help? What techniques did you use to change their point of view?

_____

_____

_____

_____

_____

_____

_____

_____

_____

_____

Thought for the week:
«Self is not merely analogous to immunity;
it is immunity.»

MONDAY ____ / ____

TUESDAY ____ / ____

WEDNESDAY ____ / ____

THURSDAY ____ / ____

FRIDAY ____ / ____

WEEKEND ____ / ____

WEEK THIRTY-THREE
DIFFERENTIATION AS AN EMOTIONAL CONCEPT

Differentiation is the lifelong process of striving to keep one's being in balance through the reciprocal external and internal processes of **self-definition** and **self-regulation**. An emotional concept, not a cerebral one, differentiation requires clear-headedness. And it has enormous consequence for new ways of thinking about leadership.

Differentiation means the capacity to become oneself out of one's self, with minimum reactivity to the position or reactivity of others. Differentiation refers more to a process than a goal that can ever be achieved.

SELF-ASSESSMENT

Differentiation is a direction in life, rather than a state of being.

○ **TRUE**   ○ **FALSE**

Obviously, differentiation has its origin in the biological notion that cells can have no identity, purpose, or distinctiveness until they have separated from their progenitors. It is a prerequisite for specialization, although it is not to be equated with similar-sounding ideas such as individuation, autonomy, or independence. Differentiation:

1. Has less to do with a person's behavior than with his or her emotional being.
2. Includes a sense of connectedness that prevents the mere gaining of distance, leaving, or cutting-off as ways to achieve it.
3. Concerns the fabric of one's existence, one's integrity.

Implicit in the biological metaphor is the idea that a self has little meaning if it cannot connect. In its simplest terms, therefore, differentiation is the capacity to be one's own integrated aggregate-of-cells person while still belonging to, or being able to relate to, a larger colony. Conversely, the capacity to think systemically and avoid the polarizations characteristic of reactivity seems to go along with the emotional growth associated with differentiation.

This concept of differentiation is a focus on strength rather than on pathology. It comes up fully on the side of personal responsibility rather than faulting the stars, society, the environment, or one's parents.

SELF-ASSESSMENT

Below is a list of qualities held by differentiated leaders. Rate your current performance in each area from 1 to 5. Identify which areas represent challenges for you, and which are strengths!

- Able to take a stand in an intense emotional system:　　(/ 5)
- Saying "I" when others are demanding "we":　　(/ 5)
- Containing your reactivity to the reactivity of others:　　(/ 5)
- Knowing where you end and others begin:　　(/ 5)
- Being clear about your own personal values and goals:　　(/ 5)
- Taking responsibility for your own emotional being:　　(/ 5)

Two final questions are worth mentioning here, one relating to morality and the other with what I shall call sabotage.

Much of the concern about strong leadership stems from a concern with morality. However, there can be no question that **strong leadership will show that morality has more to do with space than with values**, with dependency than with power. Second, most theories of leadership recognize the problems of resistance, but there is a deeper systemic phenomenon that occurs when leaders do precisely what they are supposed to do: lead. The very presence of differentiation in a leader will stir up anxious response. Yet **staying in touch with the capacity to understand and deal effectively with this system is—beyond vision, beyond perspicacity, beyond stamina—the key to the kingdom**.

Have you ever dealt with professional sabotage? What emotional processes do you imagine drive individuals to sabotage others, especially those with whom they may even share larger goals?

_____

_____

_____

_____

_____

_____

_____

_____

_____

_____

Thought for the week:

«The more accurately any system of thought can make predictions, the less room it allows for free will.»

MONDAY _____ / _____

TUESDAY _____ / _____

WEDNESDAY _____ / _____

THURSDAY _____ / _____

FRIDAY _____ / _____

WEEKEND _____ / _____

WEEK THIRTY-FOUR
TAKE FIVE

Ultimately, the relationship between risk and reality is about leadership. The Old World's process of reorientation could never have come about if that civilization had not produced individuals who were willing to go first. These "captains courageous" were not necessarily brilliant, learned, or noble. What united those who went first was desire, the capacity to be decisive, and just plain "nerve," rather than knowledge of data or technique.

To attribute these explorers' feats simply to a desire for fame and fortune not only denigrates their passion and resolve, but it also leaves out the fact that they were hardly alone among their contemporaries in those desires. What differentiates the great explorers is their "self-differentiation."

The desire to lead alone is not enough to make a great leader. One must also have courage. However, we rarely think of bravery in connection with our workplace selves. Looking back on your career so far, describe a time when you exhibited courage as a professional.

There are five aspects of their functioning that enabled these explorers to lead an entire civilization into a New World, and they are the very same factors that must be present in the leaders of any social system if it is to have a renaissance.

- A capacity to get outside the emotional climate of the day.
- A willingness to be exposed and vulnerable.
- Persistence in the face of resistance to downright rejection.
- Stamina in the face of sabotage.
- Being "headstrong" and "ruthless"—at least in the eyes of others.

What makes these attributes universal is that they are not necessarily connected to personality traits, cultural factors, or anything gender-specific. They are rather qualities that have to do with the capacity to function well when the world about you is disoriented or stuck in a certain way of thinking. They apply equally to marriage, family life, and work.

Fear of rejection has finished many great careers before they could begin. Outline a plan to put yourself out there—to be vulnerable and exposed—in the next few weeks. This may be in the form of a stretch proposal, salary negotiation discussion, or perhaps an attempt to network with someone in a desired field or position.

_____

_____

_____

_____

_____

_____

_____

_____

There are enlightening differences among leaders, particularly in terms of their ability to handle sabotage and seduction.

Exploring the coast of Florida and Labrador, Verazano was overly cautious and a perhaps a little naïve. He was petrified of going aground, and his cautiousness ironically cost him not only discoveries but eventually his life. When drawing near to an island in the Caribbean, he followed his usual habit of not getting his ship too close to shore and instead rowed in with his brother. He was promptly killed by the inhabitants. With his ship anchored so far out, his shipmates were unable to help him.

Magellan, on the other hand, was fearless beyond belief. Early in his career, when one of his ships went aground, Magellan sent another one to help but remained with his crew, staying in charge, keeping them disciplined, and maintaining the oversight necessary for the survival of their cargo and their lives. The tenacity that enabled him to accomplish one of the greatest sailing feats in history was also his downfall, however, when he allowed himself to become involved in an internecine struggle between two factions on an island, and he was killed when he interfered in the midst of a fight that was totally irrelevant to his mission.

WORD CLOUD

Are you more of a Magellan or a Verazano? Remember that a successful leader balances between risk and reality.

Magellan

Tenacious
Clear-headed
Risktaker

Verazano

Disciplined
Habit-driven
Risk averse

Thought for the week:
«One of the major limitations of imagination's fruits is the fear of standing out.»

MONDAY _____ / _____

....
....
....
....
....
....

TUESDAY _____ / _____

....
....
....
....
....
....

WEDNESDAY _____ / _____

....
....
....
....
....
....

THURSDAY _____ / _____

....
....
....
....
....
....

FRIDAY _____ / _____

....
....
....
....
....
....

WEEKEND _____ / _____

....
....
....
....
....
....

WEEK THIRTY-FIVE
COLUMBUS AS A LEADER

Columbus, in contrast, always seemed to know where he was. Not reputed to be a great chartist, he was, on the other hand, superb at "dead reckoning," the capacity to chart a course through one's own constant measurements rather than relying on the use of someone else's map—a kind of biofeedback with one's environment.

Upon his arrival at the Canary Islands on his first voyage, the reigning queen begged him to stay. But Columbus had read *The Odyssey* and knew about the Sirens. He bound himself metaphorically to his mast and responded, in effect, "Not me; I've got a job to do."

Sirens can exist outside of the sea. What potential distractions or temptations do you foresee on your path to leadership?

_____

_____

_____

_____

_____

_____

_____

_____

_____

_____

_____

_____

While all five characteristics of leadership apply, to a greater or lesser extent, to all of the navigators, Columbus is the very embodiment of them all. Not only was he one of the most imaginative men of all time, he was also one of the most determined, as well as the great example of the principle that *vision is not enough*.

Almost two millennia previously the Greeks also knew the world was round, but Columbus was the first to say, "Follow me westward as a way to go east." **To be determined, decisive, and visionary—while keeping your wits about you—may be what it takes to reorient any marriage, family, organization, society, or civilization.**

While Columbus's legacy has evolved over time, there are still many lessons to be learned from his approach to exploration. Who are the "firsts," the thought-leaders, in your industry? How have the 5 characteristics of leadership shaped their careers?

_____

_____

_____

_____

_____

_____

_____

_____

_____

_____

_____

_____

Columbus was no ordinary deck swab. He had one of the finest libraries of the time, and his imagination was rooted in the experience of history. He was excited by life. Adventure was his natural environment.

He was also a man with some savvy of how relationship systems function. It is at the very beginning of his journey that we get a hint of his capacity for understanding both the problems of leadership and the importance of self-differentiation in the leader. On the way to the canaries, the *Pinta*'s rudder broke down, and the crew seemed to have trouble fixing it. After several days, Columbus began to sense that this might be an effort to sabotage his whole venture; his colleagues' will had already waned.

Displaying an unusual awareness of the value of self-definition over efforts to coerce another, he signaled that he was going on to the Canaries by himself and would wait for them there, prepared to go on alone if he had to. He jots in his log, "I see that I'm going to have to accept what I cannot control." The *Pinta* arrived two days later.

SELF-ASSESSMENTS

I am prepared to pursue my goals alone if necessary.

○ **TRUE**   ○ **FALSE**

I accept what I cannot control.

○ **TRUE**   ○ **FALSE**

Thought for the week:
«The cost of safety is great.»

MONDAY _____ / _____

....
....
....
....
....

TUESDAY _____ / _____

....
....
....
....
....

WEDNESDAY _____ / _____

....
....
....
....
....

THURSDAY _____ / _____

....
....
....
....
....

FRIDAY _____ / _____

....
....
....
....
....

WEEKEND _____ / _____

....
....
....
....
....

WEEK THIRTY-SIX
A NEW WAY FORWARD

We must now take up Columbus's challenge. Earlier chapters were devoted to showing the emotional barriers to new thinking about relationships that keep leaders imaginatively stuck: specifically, the reliance on data, empathy, and togetherness. Now we will cross those barriers in order to help leaders out of the imaginative gridlock that characterizes the individual-model orientation of the social sciences.

We will present a view of relationships, and therefore leadership, that goes in a direction that is not only different from but sometimes opposite to the direction of traditional pathways. To suggest that gender, ethnicity, and psychological profiles are not the stuff of human relationships, or that the concentrated focus on data, method, feelings, and togetherness is misguided, can sound as counterintuitive today as it would have been in Columbus's time to say that the Earth revolves around the sun.

> Truly radical change can take a long time to penetrate the culture of its time. How have your impressions of leadership evolved over the past nine months?
>
> _____
>
> _____
>
> _____
>
> _____
>
> _____
>
> _____
>
> _____
>
> _____

The emphasis in our civilization on data, on method, on technique, and on social science categories misdirects leaders in two ways:

- First, it points them away from the reality of underlying emotional processes.
- Second, as long as emotional process is ignored, so is the sense of self, which will then undercut a leader's confidence in the uniqueness of his or her own personal being.

All this, when what our civilization needs most is leaders with a bold sense of adventure. Our nation's obsession with safety ignores the fact that **every American alive today benefits from centuries of risk-taking by previous generations**. While not all Americans share equally in that heritage, to the extent that anyone does, it is because every modern benefit from health to enjoyment to production has come about because Americans in previous generations put adventure before safety. We run the risk of becoming a nation of "skimmers" who constantly take from the top without adding significantly to its essence.

Name three past risks that you have benefitted from, either personally or professionally.

1 _____
_____
_____

2 _____
_____
_____

3 _____
_____
_____

For both families and institutions, if not our nation itself, our chronically anxious civilization inhibits well-differentiated leaders from emerging and wears down those who do. Among our reigning "Old World" superstitions are the following notions:

- Leaders influence their followers by the model they establish for identification or emulation
- The key to successful leadership is understanding the needs of one's followers
- Communication depends on one's choice of words and method of articulation
- Consensus is best achieved by striving for consensus
- Stress is due to hard work
- Hierarchy is about power

Instead, the "New World" orientation to relationships will produce a view of leadership that says the following:

- A leader's major effect on his or her followers concerns the way his or her presence affects the emotional processes in the relationship system
- A leader's major job is to understand his or herself
- Communication depends on emotional variables such as direction, distance, and anxiety
- Stress is due to becoming responsible for the relationships of others
- Hierarchy is a nature systems phenomenon rooted in the nature of protoplasm

To ponder: Do you regularly experience stress? If yes, what are your triggers?

_____

_____

_____

_____

Thought for the week:
«Even an incorrect hypothesis can lead to new ways of functioning that serendipitously stumble on the unimaginable.»

MONDAY _____ / _____

TUESDAY _____ / _____

WEDNESDAY _____ / _____

THURSDAY _____ / _____

FRIDAY _____ / _____

WEEKEND _____ / _____

WEEK THIRTY-SEVEN
SYSTEMS THINKING

The twentieth century was one of continuous surprise. The rate of change itself has seemed to change. Some of these changes have altered views that have been preserved for centuries: in physics, quantum theory, relativity, and superstring theory have exceeded previous human thought in those areas; in cosmology, the concept of the "Big Bang" has offered a far different conception of the universe.

In contrast, the social sciences have stayed true to their original concepts. The type of shift that enables one to see reality itself in a new dimension has not occurred. There have been plenty of new, innovative methods for gathering data, and the social sciences have not lacked imaginative new hypotheses. But the type of shift that enables one to see reality itself in a new dimension has not occurred. **"Soft" science has become engulfed by societal regression and gridlock to the point of becoming a faith system—that is, a system of salvation.**

What does Friedman mean when he describes our chronically anxious society as "a system of salvation"? Why would this framing be damaging to the growth of new leaders?

_____

_____

_____

_____

_____

_____

_____

_____

One major exception to this gridlock, however, is the family systems model. This model turned out to be not just a new technique for addressing family problems, but a different way of conceptualizing the human phenomenon, a new paradigm for understanding relationships. **The family systems model shifted the unity of observation from a person to a network and focused on the network principles that were universal rather than specific to culture.** Such thinking opens the door to a major reconceptualization of leadership.

Most of us are accustomed to assuming that our social and cultural attributes have played a significant role in our career development. Looking back on your professional journey, try to remove those frameworks. What do you see?

_____

_____

_____

_____

_____

_____

_____

_____

_____

_____

_____

When an organization says, "We are like a family," more is involved than closeness, togetherness, or emotional distance. Distinguishing families from other institutions is a matter of intensity, rather than of kind. Coming together is a natural process. On the other hand, there is nothing inherent in life itself that checks the togetherness forces from snuffing out individuality, except the vigilance of individuality to protect itself.

The term *system* refers to a set of interdependent variables. It recognizes society as the product, not the sum, of human relationships. What you and I can do together is far more than the addition of what you and I can do separately, and there is an awareness that this involves a different level of inquiry requiring different ways of perceiving and organizing.

The term *emotional* system refers to any group of people who have developed interdependencies to the point where the resulting system through which they are connected has evolved its own principles of organization. The structure therefore tends to influence the functioning of the system. An organizational emotional system includes the members' thoughts, feelings, emotions, fantasies, and associations, both individually and together.

The essential characteristic of systems thinking is that the functioning of any part of the network is due to its position in the network rather than to its own nature. Nature may determine the range of possible functioning and response, but not what specifically it will express.

SELF-ASSESSMENTS

I am more powerful in a system than I am acting alone.

○ **TRUE** ○ **FALSE**

My position within a network is less important to my performance than my individual attributes.

○ **TRUE** ○ **FALSE**

Thought for the week:
«Evolution requires coming together as much as it
requires the preservation of individuality.»

MONDAY ____ / ____

TUESDAY ____ / ____

WEDNESDAY ____ / ____

THURSDAY ____ / ____

FRIDAY ____ / ____

WEEKEND ____ / ____

WEEK THIRTY-EIGHT
THE NATURE OF INSTITUTIONS

Most thinking about institutions is psychodynamically oriented: relationships take their character from the personalities or backgrounds of the people involved rather than from their adaption to an overall system.

Instead, I suggest **that individuals function not out of their own personalities or past, but express that part of their nature that is regulated by the emotional process in the present system**. This applies to two factors in particular:

- Their position within relational triangles
- The forces that have been transmitted from successive generations

The models I use differ from traditional social science assumptions in three major ways. First, the model institutions' emotional processes are **self-organizing** and **multi-generational**, the forces that can be reduced to conventions of psychology, sociology, or anthropology. Relationships are not simply the product of the personalities involved, but constantly evolving structures that take shape from the adaption of each member to the adaptions others make to them in response.

Whether you are with friends, at school, or at work, the people around you matter. Have you changed systems in any realm recently (new job, new city, etc.)? How has your new environment impacted your sense of self?

_____

_____

_____

_____

_____

Second, these new models differ from traditional social science models in that they understand the past is a continuous process that goes well beyond the impact of the previous generation. The influence of the past is seen in terms of its presence rather than what has "gone by." An appropriate metaphor would be a collapsing telescope in which each cylinder overlaps, and, to some extent, continually formats the shape of the next.

What is the major ramification for leadership? **This continuous view of time enables one to see that the nature of relationships in the present has more to do with emotional processes that have been successfully reinforced for many generations than with the logic of their contemporary connection.** Institutions tend to institutionalize the pathology of the founding families, for example. Only a certain type of leadership can alter the inevitability of this "persistence of form."

To what extent are your current patterns of leadership inherited from early mentors? Are there any that should be re-evaluated? How so?

_____

_____

_____

_____

_____

_____

_____

_____

_____

_____

_____

The third way in which these new models differ is by emphasizing the *universality of life's processes.* The reason for this universality is connected to the view of time outlined above. The emotional processes that shape institutions go back to "creation," or at least to the time of the first eukaryotic cells.

This emphasis on what is similar rather than on what is different has two consequences for leadership:

- Emphasizing similarity means that the principles of leadership extend across the board to all forms of contemporary institutional life
- Shifting away from conventional traditions and toward emotional processes establishes new criteria for what information is important

The fact that family and other institutional processes run on the same current can enable leaders to improve by gaining a better understanding of how their position in their own extended family's emotional field affects their functioning.

SELF-ASSESSMENTS

Family life and work life are completely separate realms.

○ **TRUE** ○ **FALSE**

The past is past.

○ **TRUE** ○ **FALSE**

Thought for the week:
«Forces that are the most powerful in one realm are not
necessarily the most powerful in another.»

MONDAY _____ / _____

TUESDAY _____ / _____

WEDNESDAY _____ / _____

THURSDAY _____ / _____

FRIDAY _____ / _____

WEEKEND _____ / _____

WEEK THIRTY-NINE
EMOTIONAL TRIANGLES

Emotional triangles are the building blocks of any **relationship system**. They are its molecules, following their own universal laws. Triangles function predictably, irrespective of gender, class, race, culture, background, or psychological profile, and also irrespective of the relational context, the kind of business, or the nature or severity of the problem.

An emotional triangle is the manner in which the relationship between any two people, or a given individual and his or her symptoms, can be a function of an often unseen third person, relationship, or issue between them. For example:

For ten days, the Simpsons' eldest daughter lay in a hospital bed with a mysterious infection, her body unresponsive to antibiotics. During this period her parents were having the worst fight of their life over the amount of time Mr. Simpson was spending with a female colleague at work. Finally, he admitted that he was having an affair, and during a visit to the hospital he told his daughter the truth. Within forty-eight hours, her mysterious infection had mysteriously disappeared.

In the example above, which are the three sides of the emotional triangle? How is each impacting the others?

1 _____

_____

_____

2 _____

_____

_____

3 _____

_____

_____

Emotional triangles require a different level of inquiry, and they provide different criteria for what information is important. No matter who the people are or what the context, emotional triangles adhere to the following rules:

- They form out of the discomfort of people with one another
- They function to preserve themselves and oppose all intentions to change them
- They interlock in a reciprocally self-reinforcing manner
- They make it difficult for people to modify their thinking and behavior
- They transmit a system's stress to its most responsible or most focused member

Who is the most responsible member of the system in the previous example? How might the stress of the other system members impact him/her?

_____

_____

_____

_____

_____

_____

_____

_____

Observing how emotional triangles function is a way of objectifying the relationship process. Triangles make emotional processes directly observable. They demonstrate how relationship systems are self-organizing, and they support the major principle of systems thinking, that it is position rather than nature that is the key to understanding our functioning in any family or work system.

For leaders, the capacity to understand and think in terms of emotional triangles can be the key to their stress, their health, their effectiveness, and their relational binds. Almost every issue of leadership can be framed in this way, including motivation, clarity, decision-making, resistance to change, imaginative gridlock, and a failure of nerve.

Emotional triangles thus have both negative and positive effects on leaders. Their negative aspect is that they perpetuate treadmills, reduce clarity, distort perceptions, inhibit decisiveness, and transmit stress. But their positive aspect is that when a leader can begin to think in terms of emotional triangles and map diagrams of the organization, such analysis can help explain alliances and the difficulties being encountered in motivation or learning.

This in turn can help the leader get unstuck by changing emotional processes and becoming more objective about what is happening. Identifying triangles is also useful in evaluating the maturity of coworkers. It also provides a way to regulate our sensitivity so that we do not fall into the trap of empathy.

SELF-ASSESSMENT

Choose an emotional triangle in which you are the most responsible member (downmost point). Label yourself and your system members. Along the connecting side, write a word or phrase that describes each member's interaction with the person listed on the adjacent point.

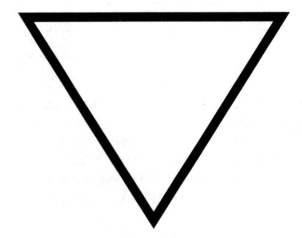

Thought for the week:
«There may be no such thing as
a two-sided relationship.»

MONDAY _____ / _____

TUESDAY _____ / _____

WEDNESDAY _____ / _____

THURSDAY _____ / _____

FRIDAY _____ / _____

WEEKEND _____ / _____

WEEK FORTY
TYPES OF EMOTIONAL TRIANGLES

As laid out in the previous week, an emotional triangle is any three members of any relationship system or any two members plus an issue or symptom. The most common emotional triangles are the following:

Type One: Family Triangles

Spouse/spouse/ any third person	child (natural or adopted), in-law, relative, boss, friend, therapist, minister, mentor, doctor, etc.
Spouse/spouse or symptom	either partner's drinking, eating, smoking, distasteful habit, health, job, hobby, credit card, etc.
Parent/child/ parent	any difference between the parents of leniency, discipline, protectiveness, freedom, individuality, etc.
Parent/child/any third person	sibling, grandparent, other relative, healer, mentor, piano teacher, soccer coach, friend(s), etc.
Parent/child/ habit	laziness, sloppiness, tardiness, carelessness, irresponsibility, lying, cheating, etc., and the issue that encompasses them all: homework

Choose one example from above that applies to your own childhood. How did the leader of the system at the time handle the issue? How would adult you, as a well-differentiated leader, address the same?

_____

_____

_____

_____

_____

Type Two: Workplace Triangles

Issues at stake:
seniority, fairness, allotment of resources, space, employee slots, benefits, working conditions, productivity, hiring and firing policies, profit-sharing, snafus and goof-ups, and management practices

Emotional triangles:
- CEO/vice president/vice president
- CEO/union/board of trustees
- CEO/profits/his or her health
- CEO/corporate culture/change
- Manager/CEO/another manager
- Manager/subordinate/superior
- Worker/manager/manager
- Worker/manager/worker
- CEO, manager, or worker/job/family
- CEO, manager, or worker/orders from above/maintaining one's integrity

From the list of issues at stake, circle the issues that are at the forefront of conflict in your organization. What is the gist of the conflict?

_____

_____

_____

_____

From the list of emotional triangles, circle the relationship triangle that is most impactful in your current workplace role. How might the triangle model help you to manage the relationship between those peoples/issues?

_____

_____

_____

Issues at stake:
payment, quality of care, expectations, boundary violations, advice, expertise

Emotional triangles:
- Mentor/mentee/symptom
- Mentor/mentee/mentee's recalcitrance
- Mentor/mentee/another mentor
- Mentor/mentee/mentee's colleague or friend
- Mentor/mentee/mentor's colleague or friend
- Mentor/mentee/another way they are connected
- Mentor/mentee/mentor's reputation
- Mentor/mentee/mentee's own intuition

Have you ever mentored someone, either officially or unofficially? What were the challenges and rewards of that experience? Do they map to any of the triangles above?

_____

_____

_____

_____

_____

_____

_____

_____

_____

_____

_____

Thought for the week:
«Triangles make emotional processes directly observable.»

MONDAY _____ / _____

TUESDAY _____ / _____

WEDNESDAY _____ / _____

THURSDAY _____ / _____

FRIDAY _____ / _____

WEEKEND _____ / _____

WEEK FORTY-ONE
THE "LAWS" OF EMOTIONAL TRIANGLES

Emotional triangles form because of the inherent instability of two-person relationships. This instability increases because of a lack of differentiation of the partners, the degree of chronic anxiety in the surrounding emotional atmosphere, and the absence of well-defined leadership. They create the illusion of intimacy. How long can any two people talk together without focusing on a third person?

This process involves more than scapegoating or finding a common enemy, however. Triangling a third person (A) *into* a relationship with B and C by agreeing to dislike (or even help) A, or triangling that third person *out* by keeping A in the dark about something they deserve to know (such as a job transfer), provides stability to B and C, who then organize themselves around the framework of the triangle. The relationship then evolves in a way that makes A, the third party, an inherent part of the connection of the other two.

Why does a secret have such power over co-conspirators? Have you ever observed this principle in action?

_____

_____

_____

_____

_____

_____

_____

_____

In families, the most obvious triangle involves an adultery, but the functioning of that triangle has more to do with how the need for secrecy creates an intense emotional bond by triangling out the other partner, A, than with the sex that is the usual focus. And even when A knows, it is the triangled-out position and the way he or she responds to the relationship of the other two (B ad C) that stabilizes or destabilizes the relationship.

Indeed, there may be no better proof that triangles are essentially an emotional process than the ways in which the intensity of B and C's extramarital relationship is governed by the way A responds to it.

SELF-ASSESSMENTS

"Love triangles" only happen on TV.

○ **TRUE**   ○ **FALSE**

The relationship between two people rarely impacts others in their orbit.

○ **TRUE**   ○ **FALSE**

Only the most powerful person in a system impacts the members of the system.

○ **TRUE**   ○ **FALSE**

Emotional triangles can also form in society itself. One way to understand this would be that from the beginning the black population of America has served as a displacement focus for the problems of white classes with one another, particularly the normal differences between classes. While these differences obviously exist and have political ramifications, they have never taken on the intensity of class struggle that occurs in other nations without a pariah group to focus on. As with families, this is not a conscious process but a self-organizing evolution that results from mutual adaptation patterns.

On the international scene, triangles are cleverly used by smaller nations to create alliances based on enmity between larger nations. Triangles were at the heart of the beginnings of World War I, the Peloponnesian War between Athens and Sparta. Triangles can also exist within the military of one country as well as between the militaries of various countries.

Emotional triangles exist on the micro-level, between individuals in an intimate system, and at the macro-level, between nations. Think big. What is the largest triangle you are part of (as a citizen, member of a religion, generation, etc.)? Map it out below.

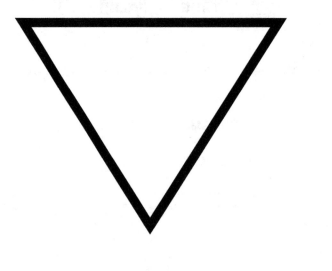

Thought for the week:
«No matter the issue over which two persons differ or who the people are, emotional triangles are regulated by the same "laws."»

MONDAY _____ / _____

TUESDAY _____ / _____

WEDNESDAY _____ / _____

THURSDAY _____ / _____

FRIDAY _____ / _____

WEEKEND _____ / _____

WEEK FORTY-TWO
HOW EMOTIONAL TRIANGLES OPERATE

Once formed, emotional triangles are **self-organizing, perpetuated by distance, and tend to be perverse**. One aspect of triangles' capacity for self-organization is the management of conflict. In most emotional triangles, one side tends to be more conflicted than the other two sides, and if one can succeed in calming that side the conflict will generally surface in one of the other relationships. Conversely, if conflict begins to erupt in one of the previously calm relationships, the previously disruptive relationship will often calm down.

An example of the former involved a woman having terrific fights with her mother-in-law. The older woman was constantly critical, and no appeals to the woman's husband to say something to his mother had any effect. However, after achieving some distance from her mother-in-law by reframing her as clownish rather than cruel, the woman reached a point where she could be amused by her antics. On her mother-in-law's next visit she responded to the usual barbs by ironically saying, "How did your son have the poor taste as to marry me?" Within an hour, the mother-in-law had ceased giving attention to the daughter-in-law and was instead embroiled in a fight with her son for not getting a better job. The two women were soon exchanging recipes.

Do you have any relationships that flare up intermittently, as above? Look for patterns that may connect that relationship to another person or issue. How can you rebalance the triangle to take stress off of the unpredictable relationship?

_____

_____

_____

_____

In the second place, *distance* also perpetuates an emotional triangle. Thus secrets and gossip that keep a person in the dark will have an avalanche effect on any community, polarizing those in and out of the secret and inhibiting communication between them.

In addition, criticism in the form of "you" statements rather than "I statements" will push people away. And if the person accepts the criticism and becomes defensive, they will become emotionally triangled into the other person's problems. The distance has the effect of creating pseudo-intimacy or alliances and always goes in the opposite direction from openness , directness, and intimacy. **If a leader can close the distance between him- or herself and the community, the leader will have a better chance of shifting the triangle, or at least making it more fluid.**

Consider the role of transparency in an organization. Many organizations both tout and fear open communication. What impact does true openness have on the emotional triangles that make up an organization?

_____

_____

_____

_____

_____

_____

_____

_____

_____

_____

_____

_____

The third characteristic of a triangle functioning is its **perversity**. The harder A works at changing the relationship of B and C, the more likely it is that their relationship will move in the opposite direction. And this will hold true no matter what position A occupies in any relationship system and no matter what B and C represent in the previous examples.

SELF-ASSESSMENT

Memory check: What are three main types of emotional triangles?

1 _____

2 _____

3 _____

This perverse characteristic of emotional triangles is important in understanding some key concepts:

- The uselessness of willing others to change
- How conflicts of will arise and destroy relationships
- Why a leader's presence is more powerful than efforts at coercion

The general rule is this: **One can only change the relationships of which one is directly a part.** If a child gets in trouble with teachers because of a particular behavior pattern, a parent will not be successful in modifying those patterns. The very act of making the attempt creates a stabilizing triangle that makes change impossible. On the other hand, the parent who works on defining "self" when the child misbehaves will have a greater success at shifting the triangle, hence modifying the pattern.

Thought for the week:
«One can only change a relationship of which
one is directly a part.»

MONDAY _____ / _____

TUESDAY _____ / _____

WEDNESDAY _____ / _____

THURSDAY _____ / _____

FRIDAY _____ / _____

WEEKEND _____ / _____

WEEK FORTY-THREE
THE INTERLOCKING NATURE OF EMOTIONAL TRIANGLES

The emotional triangles of any relationship system overlock, and in any family or work system they extend out into far-reaching super-molecules. They can extend within the same family or work system or join both; they can involve only relationship in the present; or they can be the key to how the past becomes the present.

The side that is shared by two triangles is the key to the transmission of emotional processes from one triangle to another. It is the network of interlocking triangles that accounts for the compensatory homeostatic forces that provide stability, determine communication pathways, and keeps things stuck when a leader tries to bring change.

Leaders are often advised to "leave work at work," or to keep their home life out of the office, but emotional triangles show that disconnecting those spheres is not realistic. What are some positive aspects of your home systems that can be consciously applied to your leadership?

_____

_____

_____

_____

_____

A triangle can also be with the past, and can form over several generations, as when a father is failing to discipline his own son because his harsh father beat him. The father reacts to the old triangle in his past and is unable to distinguish physical abuse and responsible discipline in the present.

It is in a family business that the concept of interlocking triangles may be both most enlightening and most helpful. They show up clearly, help explain struggle, and stress the role of the family's leader.

In corporate life, the interlocking nature of emotional triangles can cross into family life. In family business, all the tensions, alliances, and unresolved feelings that characterize the family leap over into the business and complicate decision-making processes as well as clarity. Consulting firms generally appreciate this and often give advice that will dilute the triangles, such as not having family members report directly to one another. This is again an administrative solution and will be limited in its effects.

Are you the same person in your work life and home life? How does your sense of self change in these different spheres? Remember, these two selves aren't as distinct as you may think!

_____

_____

_____

_____

_____

_____

_____

_____

_____

_____

_____

_____

_____

One of the most important interlocking emotional triangles in the world of business is that between an entrepreneur and his company's problems, on the one hand, and his position as "standard bearer" in his family of origin, on the other.

Company — Company's problems

Entrepreneur

A standard-bearer (often male, but not necessarily so) is someone who has been almost catapulted out of his or her family with a mandate to achieve. This person is usually an eldest child, or perhaps a first-born son with an uncommon drive and energy. When such people experience stress in their business, it is exponentially increased because of the importance of their succeeding for past generations. After a business failure, it is not only themselves or their immediate family and friends they feel they have failed, but also their ancestors who have been riding along since birth.

SELF-ASSESSMENT

Others are putting pressure on me to succeed.

○ **TRUE**   ○ **FALSE**

Thought for the week:
«Networks of interlocking triangles keep things stuck
when a leader tries to bring change.»

MONDAY _____ / _____

TUESDAY _____ / _____

WEDNESDAY _____ / _____

THURSDAY _____ / _____

FRIDAY _____ / _____

WEEKEND _____ / _____

WEEK FORTY-FOUR
STRESS IN EMOTIONAL TRIANGLES

leader's stress and his or her effectiveness are opposite sides of the same coin. This is not so because failure to be effective creates stress, but because the type of leadership that creates the least stress also happens to be the type of leadership that is the most effective.

The conventional view of stress is that it has to do with overwork. But if stress is simply the result of hard work or too much work, then obviously the answer to stress is not to work too hard. This is a totally unrealistic concept given the type of person who tends to wind up in leadership positions. Trying to be creative and imaginative is stressful, being responsible is stressful, maintaining vision is stressful, being on the lookout for and trying to deal with sabotage is stressful. Yet all leaders move in that direction, and not all leaders experience burnout.

If the problem of stress is simply a matter of overwork, the answer is to get away for a while, relax, do favorite things, and when you come back do not work so hard. The concept here, as with sabbaticals, is to recharge one's batteries so one can go back in and run down again.

How do we ever know when too much is enough?

How would you differentiate between stress and burnout? What role do you believe stress should play in leadership?

_____

_____

_____

_____

_____

_____

The concept of emotional triangles, however, suggests a systems view of stress. To the extent that you (A) become enmeshed in the relationship of B and C (either you have taken on the responsibility for their relationship or because they have focused on you—that is, triangled you out—as a way of achieving togetherness), you will wind up with stress for their relationship.

Obviously, everyone has limits in how much work they can handle, but the concept of an emotional triangle suggests **that the same amount of hard work will be more or less stressful depending on the position from which one approaches or becomes involved with work**. It is like lifting a heavy object: the weight alone may not be the problem, but the position from which one tries to lift it. There are limits to everyone's strength, but it takes less weight to strain your body if you attempt to lift the object from certain positions.

The stress on leaders primarily has to do with the extent to which the leader has been caught in a responsible position for the relationship of two others. They could be any two persons (family, team members, two sides to an argument) or any person or system plus a problem or goal.

Consider your own current stress levels. Would a sabbatical help? What would be waiting for you when the sabbatical was over?

_____

_____

_____

_____

_____

_____

_____

_____

_____

The way out is to make the two persons responsible for their own relationship, or the other person responsible for his or her problem, *while all still remain connected.*

It is that last phrase which differentiates de-triangling from simply quitting, resigning, or abdicating. Staying in a triangle without getting triangled oneself gives one far more power than never entering the triangle in the first place. Many charming leaders never get stressed because they intuitively stay out of triangles, but it makes them less effective.

Leaders who are most likely to function poorly physically or emotionally are those who have failed to maintain a well-differentiated position. Either they have accepted the blame owing to the irresponsibility and constant criticism of others, or they have gotten themselves into an overfunctioning position (that is, they tried too hard) and rushed in where angels and fools both fear to tread.

Well-differentiated leaders can remain in relationship with others without inheriting the negative impacts of the triangle. Like the explorers, they can hold true to their vision despite the distractions of others. Write out three self-differentiation goals for yourself in your most challenging triangle of relationships. What steps will you take to maintain your sense of self?

1 _____

_____

_____

2 _____

_____

_____

3 _____

_____

_____

Thought for the week:
«Everyone is in a triangle between his or her body and his or her mind.»

MONDAY _____ / _____

....
....
....
....
....
....

TUESDAY _____ / _____

....
....
....
....
....
....

WEDNESDAY _____ / _____

....
....
....
....
....
....

THURSDAY _____ / _____

....
....
....
....
....
....

FRIDAY _____ / _____

....
....
....
....
....
....

WEEKEND _____ / _____

....
....
....
....
....
....

WEEK FORTY-FIVE
THE TOGETHERNESS POSITION

The position that is most dangerous to a leader's health is what I call the "togetherness position," in which the leader feels responsible for keeping a system together. Such leaders are most likely to suffer burnout, function badly, or suddenly die when forces pulling in opposite directions have stretched their capacity to hold things together to its breaking point.

A study dubbed the Executive Monkey Experiment serves as a poignant metaphor (though the study has not been repeated). An effort was made to give monkeys ulcers or to promote some other kind of somatic disturbance through frustration. First, the monkey was taught how to get food and then was frustrated when it finally learned. But no amount of frustration seemed to create the desired somatic dysfunction.

Then, someone got the bright idea to make the monkey responsible for getting the food for other monkeys. This, they claimed, did produce a somatic disturbance.

SELF-ASSESSMENTS

In the example above, one member of the system feels responsible for the function of all the other members, who expect this one member to provide. Which monkey are you?

I am dependent on the inputs of another in my daily work.

○ **TRUE**   ○ **FALSE**

My daily work is driven by the needs of another.

○ **TRUE**   ○ **FALSE**

The togetherness position is one of the subtlest effects of emotional triangles—and one of the most subversive. On more than one occasion, I have seen the stress of togetherness transmitted to secretaries and subordinates who have become too emotionally involved in their bosses' problems.

On one dramatic occasion, the staff of a clinic spent their whole day processing their relationships. There was an underlying split due to the fact that a married couple who worked at the clinic had divorced, and one of the staff was now having an affair with another member of the staff. Depression and tension had split the community. The effort was made, therefore, to open dialogue among everybody.

The clinic was also staffed by a very efficient woman who took care of the administrative details. Toward the end of the day, when the consultant asked if the intensity of the situation had driven anyone to suicidal thoughts, it was the secretary who raised her hand.

The togetherness position can have a serious effects on the mental health and functioning of those who are caught up in it. What begins as an attempt to be helpful morphs into a panoply of impossible expectations. De-triangling will ease the burden. In the space below, practice setting boundaries to maintain your sense of self. State your limits.

1 _____

_____

2 _____

_____

3 _____

_____

4 _____

_____

Whenever a client of mine has developed physical symptoms of any kind while they were working on relational issues, I have always suspected triangles. I have taught them to think in threes and note where they are located, and I have helped them to de-triangle. In such cases, the symptoms have almost invariably waned, if not disappeared altogether.

There is a positive side to all this for leaders, who can use their symptoms (headaches, rashes, increased drinking) as early-warning signals that they are in an emotional triangle that is pulling, if not tearing them apart. Too often the tendency of the most aggressive leaders when they do develop symptoms is to ignore them until they get the job done. But somatic disturbances in a leader are not only warning signals but also feedback from the environment, messengers about what is going on in that relationship system.

Smart leaders listen to their bodies. What is your body telling you about the health of the organization you are currently in?

_____

_____

_____

_____

_____

_____

_____

_____

_____

_____

_____

Thought for the week:
«Leaders can use their bodies to help them
be more effective leaders.»

MONDAY ____ / ____

TUESDAY ____ / ____

WEDNESDAY ____ / ____

THURSDAY ____ / ____

FRIDAY ____ / ____

WEEKEND ____ / ____

WEEK FORTY-SIX
A CROSS-CULTURAL PHENOMENON

The notion that these principles about emotional triangles are white, male, and Western—that Japanese or Kenyan families are different in the way they discipline their children or in their concern for consensus in the business matters—is, I believe, one of the great myths of our age. I have never heard anyone from any other culture rise and say "That's not true about my family." In other words, people are always saying it is not true about *other* families.

Focusing on cultural differences inhibits a leader's capacity to be decisive. Within any culture, one rarely finds more than two-thirds of the people following all the cultural traditions. A nurse or social worker in a hospital must deal with a patient's family and help them deal with loss, failure, and the side effects of the procedure. Now how is the nurse to know in advance whether this is a Japanese family that does this or that, an Irish family, Catholic, Jewish? All this burden is eliminated when the nurse is mature enough to say, "I am going to get into the anxiety of this family and its resilience, and keep the problem in them."

SELF-ASSESSMENTS

The issues that drive chronic anxiety within systems are universal.

○ **TRUE**　○ **FALSE**

Identity is always more important than the issue at hand.

○ **TRUE**　○ **FALSE**

In order to master the principles of de-triangling, one must have a complete understanding of how triangles operate. To review, the universal aspects of emotional triangles include:

- Their interlocking nature
- Their tendency to preserve themselves
- Their distortion of perceptions
- Their creation of polarization and false alliances
- Their capacity to funnel stress toward one person

Choose two of the aspects above and write a scenario that illustrates each one. Remember that a triangle can form between any combination of three people, relationships, or issues, and that they can be formed just as easily between people, relationships, and issues of the past as they can for those of the present.

Scenario 1:

_____

_____

_____

_____

_____

Scenario 2:

_____

_____

_____

_____

_____

Emotional triangles demonstrate how self-differentiation can serve as a more powerful influence on others than any other method of motivation. These triangles are *self-organizing, interlocking,* and *perpetuated by distance.* The ability to de-triangle while remaining in relationship with the other members of the triangle empowers leaders to maintain a sense of self while still exerting influence on the other points of the triangle.

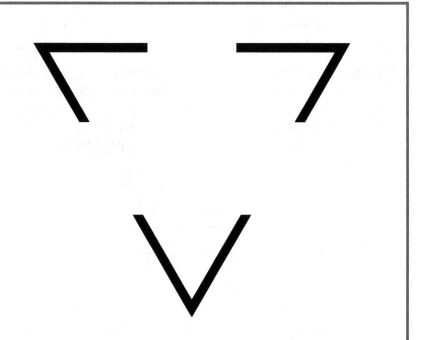

Fill in the points above. Below, detail your plan to retain your sense of self, and resist the influences of the other two points? What responsibilities can you return to their original owners?

_____

_____

_____

_____

_____

Thought for the week:
«A self is more attractive than a no-self.»

MONDAY _____ / _____

TUESDAY _____ / _____

WEDNESDAY _____ / _____

THURSDAY _____ / _____

FRIDAY _____ / _____

WEEKEND _____ / _____

WEEK FORTY-SEVEN
CONFLICTS OF WILL

Every experienced boater knows that when one is docking or pulling away, all efforts to try to overcome wind and current by simply trying harder generally do not work. Experienced sailors have learned that far better than fighting those natural forces is to position oneself so that they will, in their own natural way, aid rather than frustrate one's intent.

Similarly, physicians know that attempting to overcome disease head-on is generally a losing battle. Battles of will with viruses are generally wearying and ineffective at best. The physician will always have more success if he or she can promote the organism's own natural capacity to win and natural will to survive.

Most managers, however, have not learned this lesson. They still believe that they can teach, motivate, and inculcate values in their charges simply by exerting enough will, without due regard for the natural forces that work against such well-meaning efforts but which can be harnessed to the leader's helm.

SELF-ASSESSMENTS

Trying harder is not the answer to every problem.

○ **TRUE**   ○ **FALSE**

Force of will is directly proportional to the size of a leader's sphere of influence.

○ **TRUE**   ○ **FALSE**

The factor that is almost always present in relationship systems that are deeply disturbed, if not disintegrating, is a **conflict of will**.

This conflict is sometimes blatantly contentious and sometimes subtly masked by charm or passive obstinacy. Similarly, conflict of will is always present in the failure of teachers, counselors, and consultants to make headway against the riptides of resistance that run counter to their intent. It goes without saying that when continued efforts by CEOs, managers, and administrators are producing little to no progress, they are probably swimming against the tide. Conflict of will is no way to get the results one wants.

How then, does one go with the flow and still take the lead?

Answer: **by positioning oneself in such a way that the natural forces of emotional life carry one in the right direction**. The key to that positioning is the leader's own self-differentiation, by which I mean his or her capacity to be:

- A non-anxious presence
- A challenging presence
- A well-defined presence
- A paradoxical presence

Are there any "forces of will" at conflict in your organization currently? Does the conflict tend to stay self-contained? What is the impact of these clashing wills on the surrounding teams?

_____

_____

_____

_____

_____

_____

_____

Differentiation is not about being coercive, manipulative, reactive, pursuing, or invasive; **it is about being rooted in the leader's own sense of self rather** than focused on his or her followers.

Although it may be perceived this way by those who are not taking responsibility for their own being, self-differentiation is not "selfish." Furthermore, the power inherent in a leader's presence does not reside in physical or economic strength but in the nature of his or her own being, so that even when leaders are entitled to great power by dint of their office, it is ultimately the nature of their presence that is the source of their real strength.

Leaders function as the immune systems of the institutions they lead—not because they ward off enemies but because they supply the ingredients for the system's integrity.

It can be difficult to separate a leader from his or her trappings of office. Think of a leader that you admire, whether in your professional sphere, or in another, such as politics, sports, or activism. Subtract the rights conferred by their established position. What is the true source of their leadership?

_____

_____

_____

_____

_____

_____

_____

_____

_____

_____

Thought for the week:
«Most leaders don't recognize what every sailor knows:
fighting natural forces is ineffective
and leads to burnout.»

MONDAY ____ / ____

TUESDAY ____ / ____

WEDNESDAY ____ / ____

THURSDAY ____ / ____

FRIDAY ____ / ____

WEEKEND ____ / ____

WEEK FORTY-EIGHT
THE POWER OF PRESENCE

The notion that an entity can modify surrounding relationships through its presence rather than its forcefulness is not unknown to science. Catalysts work that way: *to catalyze* refers to a reaction that occurs without forcibly rearranging the parts. But perhaps a transformer in an electrical circuit is the best metaphor for the workings of presence.

Transformers can activate or deactivate a circuit that runs through them, depending on the number of coils they contain. For example, one side of the transformer has six coils, the other two; this is a three-to-one transformer. If you send the current in from the two to the six it will triple; send it the other way and it will be reduced to a third of its former strength. **Reactive leaders function as a step-up transformer.** As one education administrator said, "My mother was a step-up transformer, all right. If there was anxiety in the room and she was present, you could count on it escalating. It went into her at 110 and came out at 11,000."

Are there any step-up "transformers" in your life? Describe a time when their tendencies disproportionately escalated a situation. Did you stay calm, or get caught up in the storm?

_____

_____

_____

_____

_____

_____

_____

_____

But **it is also possible to be a step-down transformer**—to function in such a way that you let the current through you without zapping you or fusing you to the rest of the circuit. This is not easy, and yet it is within the capability of most leaders. It has far more to do with their presence than with their actions.

Part of the difficulty in making the conceptual leap from action to presence is that all leaders, parents, or presidents have been trained to do something—that is, to fix it. This is due to the emphasis on the cognitive aspects of the brain, the resulting emphasis on method and technique, and the anxious atmosphere of contemporary society. To the extent that leaders and consultants can maintain a non-anxious presence in a highly energized anxiety field, **they can have the same effects on that field that transformers have in an electrical circuit**.

Transformers reduce the potential in a field by the nature of their own presence and being; they are in effect a field themselves. This is not a matter of breaking a circuit"; anyone can remain non-anxious if they also try to be non-present. The trick is to be both non-anxious and present simultaneously.

Revisit the event you described in the last exercise. What actions could you have taken to de-escalate the situation?

_____

_____

_____

_____

_____

_____

_____

_____

_____

_____

Leadership that is rooted in a sense of presence can also be misconstrued as a justification for passivity—for avoiding getting your feet wet, for just being "nice so everyone will love you." It can also lead to mistaken notions that data and method are unimportant, that the bottom line does not matter, or that outcome is irrelevant and the approach, therefore, impractical.

Leadership through self-differentiation is not easy; learning techniques and imbibing data are far easier. Nor is striving or achieving success as a leader without pain: there is the pain of loneliness, the pain of personal attacks, the pain of losing friends.

That is what leadership is about.

Many believe that leadership is about power, popularity, or control. Well-differentiated leadership is different. Reflecting on what you have learned, write a personal definition of leadership. What is leadership to you?

Leadership is:

_____

_____

_____

_____

_____

_____

_____

_____

_____

_____

_____

_____

Thought for the week:
«Anyone can remain non-anxious if
they also try to be non-present.»

MONDAY ____ / ____

_____
_____
_____
_____
_____
_____

TUESDAY ____ / ____

_____
_____
_____
_____
_____
_____

WEDNESDAY ____ / ____

_____
_____
_____
_____
_____
_____

THURSDAY ____ / ____

_____
_____
_____
_____
_____
_____

FRIDAY ____ / ____

_____
_____
_____
_____
_____
_____

WEEKEND ____ / ____

_____
_____
_____
_____
_____
_____

WEEK FORTY-NINE
LEADERSHIP THROUGH
SELF-DIFFERENTIATION

In the first few months of 1990, I began to experience two different sets of physical symptoms, each of which suggested the need for surgery. One was severe chest pain accompanying any intense physical exercise; the other was a recurring tingling and numbness in my left leg and arm. Tests indicated the need for angioplasty to unclog one of my arteries, lest I experience a heart attack. At the same time, tests of my right carotid artery indicated the need to unclog that artery lest I experience a stroke. The problem was which operation to undergo first, since either procedure would jeopardize the other organ, bringing about exactly what the other procedure was designed to prevent.

What I came to realize after I had worked my way through this crisis was that my experience was a metaphor for the handling of any crisis anywhere, and that major principles could be drawn from my personal experience for helping any leader.

The principles of well-differentiated leadership are just as powerful in personal spheres as they are in professional ones. What is a non-work-related area of your life that needs the attention of a leader (you)?

_____

_____

_____

_____

_____

It was probably this personal experience of the need to be a leader in my own life at that moment that helped me understand what I have said above. It was also a test of my own hypotheses. There is little question in my mind that my capacity to navigate the narrow passage left open to my future existence has affected my leadership capacity in all other endeavors since.

I worked my way through my health dilemma using the leadership principles for enduring crisis, touching on every issue of leadership discussed so far:

- The management of information
- The management of relationships
- The management of anxiety
- The management of self

All during this period I was helped immensely by two close friends, both in the medical field, who were able to funnel additional information to me about both procedures. They also helped with their humor, and with reminders of the addictiveness of information and the fallaciousness of expertise. I found they had just the right distance.

SELF-ASSESSMENTS

If a leader can't do it alone, they shouldn't do it at all.

○ **TRUE** ○ **FALSE**

A leader's job is to manage people, not information.

○ **TRUE** ○ **FALSE**

In leading myself through this crisis, I tried to employ several principles. I was less aware that they were principles at the time; instead, my functioning seemed to come from what I believed about how organisms respond, the importance of a non-anxious presence, and what can be learned through interaction and relationships.

Friedman's theories of leadership stem from his own experiences overcoming challenges. Are there any personal principles that you have drawn from your own life? What experiences shaped them?

_____

_____

_____

_____

_____

_____

_____

_____

_____

_____

_____

_____

_____

_____

_____

_____

_____

Thought for the week:
«All leadership begins with the management
of one's own health.»

MONDAY _____ / _____

TUESDAY _____ / _____

WEDNESDAY _____ / _____

THURSDAY _____ / _____

FRIDAY _____ / _____

WEEKEND _____ / _____

WEEK FIFTY
MANAGEMENT

MANAGEMENT OF INFORMATION

As I have said, information and expertise does not take the place of making decisions. One wants to make informed decisions, but if "being informed" takes over, reliance on expertise can complicate matters. Experts are not always clear with you about what is a fact, what is a hypothesis, and what is a finding. Findings based on a particular research methodology might produce other or even contrary results to findings based on a different methodology. I learned to be wary of those who were too sure.

The biggest issue regarding the management of information is this: **when should you conclude that you have enough?**

Perpetually waiting on others allows a leader to avoid choosing a path. Consider your current responsibilities – is there a decision you have been putting off making? In the space below, weigh your options, then make a choice. If you wait for the perfect time to act, you will never act at all.

_____

_____

_____

_____

_____

Even though I had heard several opinions, I was the one who was responsible for making a choice. You must not let the fact that the experts know more than you rob you of your responsibility to be decisive. I learned to handle this issue by the rule that whenever the same question asked several times in a row to various experts brought no new information, it was time to stop gathering the facts.

MANAGEMENT OF THE RELATIONSHIP SYSTEM

I had had enough experience working with physicians to know that as competent as any physician might be, everyone has ups and downs, prejudices, relational binds, and vulnerabilities. They also have other relationships with each other: joint business ventures, memberships in the same club, church, or synagogue; children in the same class or on opposing soccer teams. It has always seemed important to me, therefore, to pay attention to the relational networks of physicians and me, including their relationships with one another. Not only might this contribute to the desired outcome, it would also keep me out of triangles and not affect my own clarity.

The most obvious triangle (me, my heart, my brain) was the initial one with which I navigated my way through cardiology and neurology, all the different specialties, information-gathering, and so on. Other triangles included my neurologist, cardiologist, vascular surgeons, cardiac surgeon, arteriogram technician, internist, and orthopedic surgeon. In every case, I was the "A" position—the apex—of the triangle.

SELF-ASSESSMENTS

One's position in a system is more important than one's individual characteristics.

○ **TRUE** ○ **FALSE**

The best way to avoid the negative impacts of an emotional triangle is to avoid triangles altogether.

○ **TRUE** ○ **FALSE**

MANAGEMENT OF ANXIETY

In one sense, this entire story is about the management of anxiety, where injecting humor and keeping things loose is important.

During my health crisis, I a close relative became very anxious about my condition and phoned daily to find out the latest results. No matter what I did to reassure her, she kept coming up with other possibilities. Finally, one day I decided to loosen things up by **reversing the flow of anxiety**. When she called that evening I proceeded to exaggerate all my symptoms and give a horrendously gory idea of what the future entailed. There was a complete silence for a minute, then she asked, "C'mon, what did you really find out?" From that point on, she stopped being pessimistic, and I no longer had her haunting doubts to contend with.

In any emotional triangle, information can flow in all directions, but tends to pool at the feet of the most responsible member of the system, as in the example above. Reversing this flow can prevent a leader from becoming overwhelmed, losing focus, and experiencing burnout. Where in your life is the most unwelcome information flowing from currently? What steps can you take to reverse the flow?

_____

_____

_____

_____

_____

_____

_____

_____

_____

Thought for the week:
«The looser your presence is, the looser everyone's
relationship will be with you and one another.»

MONDAY _____ / _____   **TUESDAY** _____ / _____

WEDNESDAY _____ / _____   **THURSDAY** _____ / _____

FRIDAY _____ / _____   **WEEKEND** _____ / _____

WEEK FIFTY-ONE
TIMES OF CRISIS

In a sense, everything I have described up to this point could be listed under the title of "Management of Self": the effort to remain clear, the management of my own anxiety, the effort to remain out of triangles, the determination to be responsible and decisive. **But there is another dimension that is simply about me and myself—perhaps another triangle.**

On one occasion, I almost lost it. The anxiety in my family and the numerous questions being asked about whether I was sure I was doing the right thing began to get to me. I began to wonder if I had put in too much effort, or if I had missed something, and began to regress into precisely the attitudes that I had so proudly avoided. I awoke at four in the morning ruminating about the danger, the loss of the future.

I left the house and went down to the ocean. Standing on the beach beneath the stars, with the waves licking my sandals, I remembered how Columbus looked across the sea in the direction he had come from. And I got back in touch with that essence of adventure that I had been writing about.

A leader's most important relationship is to him- or herself. It's been nearly a year since you started this leadership journey. Take a moment to check in. Do you still feel the sense of adventure that motivated you to pick up this volume in the first place? If yes, where are you headed? If not, where do you think you lost it?

_____

_____

_____

_____

_____

Another method of self-regulation I practiced was deep breathing. Biofeedback specialists have found that like meditation or prayer, deep breathing can keep you focused on yourself, and it has the additional advantage of oxygenating the blood.

> This exercise works best off the page. Grab an article or watch a few videos on deep breathing. Implement this practice daily if you can, but especially in times of stress, when an emotional triangle is starting to get to you, or the burden of responsibility starts to feel too heavy. It will help.

To summarize the principles of leadership in times of crisis:

- Keep up your functioning; don't let crisis become the axis around which your world resolves
- Develop a support system outside of the work system
- Stay focused on long-term goals
- Practice deep breathing, prayer, or meditation
- Listen to your body
- Watch the triangles
- Work out the balance between being responsible for self and being labeled obstreperous
- Keep the system loose through humor
- It's time to make decisions when the same question brings no new information
- Accept the possibility that your own functioning brought the crisis on, which means that you may be able to influence recuperation

The table below further illustrates the tensions that leaders face in managing themselves during periods of crisis. There is no "right" answer to the question of how to find the correct balance between these opposing stances; all one can say is that to the extent that the leader has been continually working at self-differentiation, he or she is more likely to avoid the extremes.

The key to self-regulation in crisis is 1) understanding that it is appropriate to go in different directions at different times and 2) being able to go in one direction or the other without triggering a counterbalancing reaction.

A leader's most important relationship is to him- or herself. It's been nearly a year since you started this leadership journey. Take a moment to check in. Do you still feel the sense of adventure that motivated you to pick up this volume in the first place? If yes, where are you headed? If not, where do you think you lost it?

Tensions in Leadership During Crisis

Lean on others	⟷	Stay accountable
Get information	⟷	Be decisive
Keep distance	⟷	Stay connected
Do not avoid	⟷	Do not try to solve
Keep up functioning	⟷	Refrain from avoiding or denying
Maintain commitment to see it through	⟷	Do not let it become the axis of life
Be willing to chances	⟷	Regulate reactivity
Work at being objective	⟷	Honor perversity
Appreciate loneliness	⟷	Do not cut off
Stay in triangles	⟷	Do not get triangled

Thought for the week:
«If there is a moment of truth in leadership, it is amid crisis.»

MONDAY _____ / _____

TUESDAY _____ / _____

WEDNESDAY _____ / _____

THURSDAY _____ / _____

FRIDAY _____ / _____

WEEKEND _____ / _____

WEEK FIFTY:TWO
A YEAR IN REVIEW

In our final pages, let's revisit key principles of leadership:

SOCIETY

- Regressed institutions will always exhibit chronically anxious characteristics—reactivity, herding, blaming, a quick-fix mentality, and lack of well differentiated leadership
- The underlying causes in an imaginatively gridlocked society will be emotional, not cerebral
- A major criterion for judging the anxiety level of any society is its loss of playfulness
- Society must balance the conflict between the natural forces of togetherness and self-differentiation

RELATIONSHIPS

- It is easier to be the least mature member of a highly mature system than the most mature member of a very immature system
- Increasing one's pain tolerance for others helps them mature
- Stress and burnout are primarily due to getting caught in a responsible position for others and their problems
- The more anxious you are to see that something is done, the less motivated your partner will be to take the lead

SELF

- Stamina, resolve, remaining connected, the capacity for self-regulation of reactivity, and having horizons beyond what one can see is essential
- There is no way out of a chronically painful system except by being willing to go through a temporarily more acutely painful phase
- People who are cut off from relationship systems do not heal
- Most decisions turn out right or wrong because of the way we act after making the decision

WELL-DIFFERENTIATED LEADERSHIP

- Focuses on strength
- Is concerned for one's own growth
- Works with motivated people
- Matures the system
- Seeks enduring change
- Is concerned to define self (takes stands)
- Is fed up with the treadmill
- Looks at one's own stuckness
- Is challenged by difficult situations
- Recognizes that reactivity and sabotage are evidence of one's effectiveness
- Has a universal perspective
- Sees problems as the focus of preexisting anxiety
- Adapts towards strength
- Has a challenging attitude that encourages responsibility
- Is more likely to create intimate relationships

On the third day of Creation, just before all forms of life were about to multiply, the Holy One said to his creatures:

> I see that what some of you treasure most is survival, while what others yearn for most is adventure. So I will give you each a choice. If what you want most is stability, then I will give you the power to regenerate any part you lose, but you must stay rooted where you grow. If, on the other hand, you prefer mobility, you may also have your wish, but you will be more at risk. For then I will not give you the ability to regain your previous form.

Those that chose stability we call trees, and those that chose opportunity became animals.

Write yourself three new goals for the year to come. Embrace the adventures ahead.

1 _____

_____

_____

_____

2 _____

_____

_____

_____

3 _____

_____

_____

_____

Thought for the week:
«Just because a pager is torn off the calendar does not mean that unit of time has ceased to exist.»

MONDAY _____ / _____

....
....
....
....
....

TUESDAY _____ / _____

....
....
....
....
....

WEDNESDAY _____ / _____

....
....
....
....
....

THURSDAY _____ / _____

....
....
....
....
....

FRIDAY _____ / _____

....
....
....
....
....

WEEKEND _____ / _____

....
....
....
....
....